Judy Prescott is a widow of five years. a mother to two adult children and grandmother to six grandsons. Originally from Bristol, England, she has lived in South Wales for 35 years. She enjoys writing, now retired, and spends time with her grandchildren.

Judy Prescott

A SISTERLY ADVENTURE

ON THEIR TRAVELS AGAIN

AUSTIN MACAULEY PUBLISHERS
LONDON * CAMBRIDGE * NEW YORK * SHARJAH

Copyright © Judy Prescott 2025

The right of Judy Prescott to be identified as author of this work has been asserted by the author in accordance with sections 77 and 78 of the Copyright, Designs and Patents Act 1988.

All rights reserved. No part of this publication may be reproduced, stored in a retrieval system, or transmitted in any form or by any means, electronic, mechanical, photocopying, recording, or otherwise, without the prior permission of the publishers.

Any person who commits any unauthorised act in relation to this publication may be liable to criminal prosecution and civil claims for damages.

All of the events in this memoir are true to the best of author's memory. The views expressed in this memoir are solely those of the author.

A CIP catalogue record for this title is available from the British Library.

ISBN 9781035851836 (Paperback)
ISBN 9781035851843 (ePub e-book)

www.austinmacauley.com

First Published 2025
Austin Macauley Publishers Ltd®
1 Canada Square
Canary Wharf
London
E14 5AA

Chapter One

'What do we do now?' Jackie asked her sister, Claire. A tinge of laughter escaped from her mouth as she uttered the words, despite being concerned.

Family holidays with the two sisters, their spouses and their offspring was always a talking point. Tweaking schedules and not normal holiday activities was always par for the course. Remembering the occurrences only ever relevant to Jackie and company would always be an interesting, comical conversation, coupled with laughter for everyone concerned, lots of it.

Nothing had changed over the years, and the holiday mode was at it again in full swing! The only difference was that Jackie and Claire were the only two experiencing the holiday cum wedding invitation extravaganza this time. Booking.com should have guaranteed an overnight stay without any surprises. Wrong! The photographs of the hotel cum public house should have ensured a peaceful night's sleep, in readiness for a flight from Gatwick airport to Canada the following afternoon; "should have" being the ever-important words.

Arriving outside the accommodation in preparation for the next day, and seeing the place in total darkness was bad enough, but finding no door open or a reception to check into had all concerned as to what was going to happen next. At ten-fifteen in the evening, the skies now devoid of any sunlight, sleeping in the car appeared to be the next step forward. Where were they going to find accommodation at that time in the evening elsewhere?

The building, a 15th-century olde-worlde place, steeped in history, looked interesting from the outside. With no straight lines, unevenly shaped walls and ceilings; misshaped roofing levels and sloping floors, all obvious and apparent looking through the glass in the front door entrance. The door was locked but evidence of light was seen at the rear of the property and a few of the upstairs windows. But how were they to get inside the building? Questions, questions, and yet more questions.

It was dark outside, but a passer-by was stopped and asked about whether any entrance to the public house was accessible. His response had been productive and climbing the slightly dangerous fire escape stairs at the side of the building was taken with trepidation. Somehow, Jackie doubted that an attempt to climb the stairs with a walking stick in tow should have actually been taken at all. But needs must, and she managed them eventually.

The doorway was low, and at a mere 5ft 1inch in height for both of them, they'd not bumped their heads; well, not yet anyway. The wonky, uneven floorboards creaked as they both walked the corridor, unsure as to where they were actually heading. Closed door after closed door was passed by until they had come to a dead end and reverted down the now familiar corridor once again.

Heading towards another corridor, one with equally creaky floorboards and low beamed ceilings, they'd both bent their heads to avoid any impending bumps. A set of stairs led to a floor below, so Claire climbed down them, leaving Jackie standing at the top. A voice echoed that Claire had found the reception area, locked!

The characters Stan Laurel and Oliver Hardy had come to mind, a comedy duo act during the early classical Hollywood era of American cinema. Englishman Stan Laurel and American Oliver Hardy started their career as a duo in the silent film era, later on successfully transitioning to "talkies". Stan Laurel's signature piece was to ruffle his hair with his hands as a sign of uncertainty and confusion, echoing the words "What do we do now?".

Jackie and Claire were right there alongside them, asking the same question. Luckily, a gentleman walked out of a room and into the corridor they were occupying, both looking mesmerised and completely lost, and the conversation had unfolded crucial information. The owner/worker had left the building some two hours earlier and both sisters were told that there were no other staff members on the premises; in fact, the owner/worker was the *only* staff member in charge of the hotel cum public house! He was running it completely solo.

Money, apparently, was tight. Ouch, horror had crept in, along with anxious looks from both ladies. With a telephone number given by the gentleman, Claire proceeded to ring the number given, thanking him for his help. The sisters were alone again. Good monies had been fully paid for the accommodation in advance. Had they been taken for a ride? Scammed even?

The staff member (owner?) arrived some ten minutes later. A scruffily dressed elderly gentleman, who hastily retreated to the locked reception room and emerged with two keys. Handing them to Claire, he quickly left the building. Two anxious people, after noting the room numbers on the keyrings, slowly made their way to the locked doors the keys would open, hopefully. Neither of them were convinced.

The room on the top floor, although clean and tidy, was an eye-opener. Something not expected at all; Claire's grimace had said it all. The four-poster bed had seen much better days and was way too big for the average-sized room it had occupied. Any chance of watching the television in the room would have been hampered by the thick mesh curtain covering the bed itself. Not that either of them had any interest in turning the television on.

Did it actually work? That was another question. A debatable one, at that. Sleep was on the agenda, first and foremost.

The bathroom door was opened to yet another unexpected encounter. A suite of burnt orange confronted them with matching accessories, ceramic tiles and bright orange paintwork; the bath itself installed higher from the floor than usual, as Jackie had experienced a short while later. With no handle bars to hold onto, or a slip-proof bath mat in evidence, she could easily have broken her neck or any other part of her body for that matter, when getting out of it.

Thankfully, nothing of that nature had occurred. Desperate for a bath on reaching the accommodation, Jackie wouldn't have put herself through the pandemonium of getting in or out of it, otherwise. She so wished she had bathed at her sister's bungalow before starting the journey. Hindsight is a wonderful thing! Jackie had drawn the short straw. Claire hadn't wanted to sleep in the four-poster bed and had taken the second room allocated, where a standard double bed had sufficed the room.

The bathroom amenities there, although still an antiquated 1980s-coloured suite, were far less severe than those in Jackie's room.

Cups had been laid out on a bedside table in both rooms, laden with teabags, sugar and coffee bags; no milk cartons though. A mad dash was made by Claire to the petrol station opposite, where a disposable cup full of milk was given as they'd closed their doors for the evening. A more than grateful cup of tea was similar to nectar to the Gods; not even a stiff whisky could match it. A cup of tea was a must, therapeutic and calming, where Jackie was concerned anyway.

Claire, on the other hand, preferred coffee, but both beverages couldn't be drunk without milk. It was time to try and get some sleep, some shut-eye. Tomorrow was another day.

The morning emerged far too quickly, and as expected, no staff members were around. The reception door was closed and in total darkness. Neither Claire nor Jackie was surprised; their holiday had continued as it had started, disastrously. No breakfast to be had there then! Jackie placed her room key on the floor near the reception door, where it could be seen when the supposedly same scruffy gentleman had decided to make an appearance.

Claire, being the more daring of the two siblings, hid her key in one of the bedside table's drawers as she'd walked out of it with her overnight belongings. 'Let him look for it,' she'd said mischievously.

To be fair, the welcome, or not as it had turned out, wasn't impressive. With their monies paid beforehand, why should he get away with what had occurred the evening before? He had though, but Claire had made it difficult for him to locate the door key to the room she'd occupied the evening before. Crafty smiles bestowed their faces as they walked out of the premises; a different staircase to the one they had entered the evening before, thankfully. Jackie hadn't needed her walking stick, a definite plus.

The premises, a boarding house for the less privileged it appeared, were in a total state of disrepair. So sad in reality, as the building could have more than paid for itself, with the restaurant and bar, along with living accommodations on the upper floor. A historic building needing tender loving care from someone to bring it back to life. Who knew the reasoning behind the dilapidated state, both inside and out, but Jackie, for one, had almost cried.

She'd loved older premises and a 15th century public house required keeping, for historic reasons at best.

Booking.com should have held their heads up in shame, but the priority for the sisters now was to continue their journey to Canada as planned. A learning curve, definitely; they'd suffered worse on their life's encounters and put things to the back of their minds for now and into perspective. Their stomachs were rumbling, along with a thirst requiring quenching.

Thankfully, a quick walk around the corner had discovered a greasy spoon cafe, small and quaint. It would do. Nothing could replicate where they had just walked away from, could it?

A large mug of tea was ordered for Jackie and a strong coffee for Claire. Toast was added, purely to put some sustenance in their bodies before reaching Gatwick airport; a more substantial meal could be afforded then. It was important to reach the airport with plenty of time to spare; time was of the essence.

Claire, without thinking, dabbed Jackie's teabag into her already prepared coffee after the waitress had brought their beverages to their table. Toast and jam, Marmite for Jackie, was to follow shortly afterwards, they were politely informed. The sisters' faces, somewhere between grimaces of despair and quiet chuckles, were euphoric. Jackie quickly picked up the coffee/tea concoction and asked the waitress for a replacement, for which she had obliged without question.

As they got into the car for the onward journey ahead, who knew what was in store for them? Assumptions aside, this was Jackie and Claire on their holidays again and anything could happen. Guessing?... There was absolutely no point. What will be, will be! If anything could ever run smoothly for them, it would be a miracle in the making, for certain.

Jackie and Claire were beginning a more than eventful two-plus weeks of adventure, away from the UK; Canada, no less. Only time would tell the story of their impending holiday cum wedding invitation; whatever, it would be a journey out of the norm, that was for sure. Sisters, Jackie and Claire, were the people travelling and nothing was going to be straightforward. No question about it. An easy ride was never par for the course, and they had only just started.

Chapter Two

Jackie, being a cautious and sometimes nervous driver, had restricted her travels to local areas as a rule. The motorway lanes were daunting at times, which is when the nerves kicked in for her. An endless two-lane dual carriageway drive was dealt with easily enough though, with no tempers frayed. Jackie's usually mild-mannered speech did let her down badly occasionally, when driving, with swearing expletives from behind the wheel. Not good at all.

Unknown places and new territories were her downfall, always. Driving to areas not visited beforehand had put the collywobbles in Jackie, causing extra nervousness and uncertainty. Her confidence would become depleted. Alan would always drive her to new places the day before, enabling Jackie to at least view the area she would be travelling alone.

He wasn't available to do it any more, leaving her outside her comfort zone at times. A nervous wreck Alan would have called it, whilst laughing. Jackie could see him now, doing just that.

Until her late husband's passing, some four years back, motorway driving had become a no-go area; something her mind had absolutely prohibited. Alan had always driven wherever a motorway was required, Jackie predominantly navigating him. They'd often taken the wrong turning and a mystery tour prevailed before reaching their final destination a little later, and sometimes a lot later than anticipated.

There were a lot of them, wrong turnings that were made, but wrong turnings had often discovered parts of the country not noted on the map. Hidden areas of beauty, with rippling streams and picturesque fields full of pretty flowers, were tranquil beauty spots that they would otherwise have completely overlooked and missed out on. Jackie and Alan had crammed lots of travelling into their lives before the inevitable illnesses had reared their ugly heads.

Living it was called, and normal to all who were here to tell their stories. Alan's may have ended but the memories were still there. Many of the past holiday experiences were taken with Claire and her partner of over twenty years, John. All had included small, mediocre, or larger catastrophes along the way. Tales to pass to children and grandchildren, and hopefully, in Jackie's case, great-grandchildren. Hurdles were there to climb over, and climb over them they did.

Jackie's need for travelling had forced her to confront her fears and drive the motorways she'd hated and despised. Claire hadn't ever passed her driving test, so the journey to Gatwick airport was taken very cautiously. John had always travelled happily behind the wheel, leaving Claire to nod off here and there along the way. 'Do not go to sleep, Claire,' Jackie had told her. 'We will never get there otherwise.' She meant it.

The train or National Express coach was so much simpler in Jackie's eyes. Why was she putting herself through this? Why indeed? A family wedding in Canada, no less; a glance at the huge country and its fine views, the scenery at its best.

She calmed down at the thought and concentrated on her destination. How many more roundabouts were there? The drive seemed never-ending. She just wanted to get there, before the journey had even begun.

Jackie parked the car easily enough in the long-stay car park that had been paid for days earlier, online of course. How else do you pay for things these days? Removing the luggage from the boot of the vehicle, both girls missed the men. Where were they when they were needed most? Lifting a mere suitcase realised the requirements of their partners; ladies they were, weren't they?

Sadly, Alan was now resting in peace, even though Jackie knew that he would have preferred being the bob-a-job man everyone had relied on for something or other. He was in his element with a pair of working jeans on, full of rips and holes, dried-up plaster, paint and oil stains. Knee deep in mud, or the equivalent, and working from dawn until midnight, seven days a week. That was Alan in a nutshell, on the go all the time.

John was working away; he worked away a lot. His career had taken him all over the world, a master in the expertise of motorcycles. Repairs, lecturing, and being part of the teams' pit stop involved in motorcycle races, amateur and professional. The girls had been left on their own this time, to their own devices. Should they have been, though? Things hadn't started out that brilliantly, but no bones had been broken, not yet any roads.

Pulling the suitcases behind them, Claire endeavoured to hand in the car keys, returning with a ticket to present on their return. 'Don't lose it,' she muttered to herself. Losing, or rather misplacing, similar tickets in the past had been somewhat a regular occurrence. Both on Claire's and Jackie's travels, whether together or on separate holidays, the elusive car parking ticket wasn't always readily available. Now where did they put it? Somewhere safe, obviously; too safe apparently.

The shuttle bus would take them to the airport, free of charge, and then their journey would begin. It had been a while since either of them had flown abroad, their minds a little rusty but aside from the newfound machines taking the place of real human beings, eventful it was going to be. Gatwick and Heathrow were large airports, and the likes of Bristol and Cardiff were so much less complicated. Canada was off the grid for the smaller airports, so Gatwick it was; like it or lump it.

'The quicker we're on that plane, the better,' Jackie commented to a nervous Claire. Claire didn't fly well and a long-haul flight deemed her more anxious than usual. John wasn't there to comfort her either. Jackie would do her best on that score but she was not a substitute for Claire's long-term partner. She knew that all too well. Alan was so missed, but he couldn't be there with Jackie either, not in body (maybe in spirit).

Flustered faces had eventually accomplished what was required. Their luggage was now safely on the conveyor belts, heading for Toronto, then on to Calgary. Having to catch a connection between stops in Canada was something not appreciated, but necessary. A direct flight initially booked was, by the airline itself, switched to a connection at Toronto before reaching the destination required, being Calgary airport.

An extra four hours travelling by air was Claire's worst nightmare, but sadly, completely unavoidable. Both of them wanted to attend the wedding, a family member on John's side but known to Jackie from a small boy. Mark was now a thirty-something adult entering marriage for the first time. Emigrating from the UK to Canada, he'd met his sweetheart in Wales whilst attending university there. She'd studied there too, as an exchange student from Canada.

Entering the departure lounge, huge as it was, duty-free browsing was a must. With Jackie, browsing it usually was; monies were needed whilst on holiday, rather than before they'd left the UK. Thrifty she was, and always would be. Jackie's nature at best, checking price tags before deciding whether to purchase items. If they appeared too pricey, then they remained on the shelves.

A notebook caught her eye, nothing special, just a small jotter for her sometimes vivid imagination; maybe to keep count of her finances, now dwindling drastically. Jackie was approaching state pension age and retirement, the pennies required constant checks and updates. Bills paid, first and foremost; well before treating herself. Being part of a large family had taught her to be careful on the money front, sometimes a little too careful.

A glum look confirmed a high price for a mere notebook until the back page had mentioned the name of the designer of the item. Milly Green, that was her mother's name! Her late mother had remarried, causing her surname to change, but Milly Green she was for more than twenty-five years. Jackie bought the notebook, disregarding the price tag. Wonders would never cease! She was allowed to have a wobble at times.

Claire, being a smoker, would always check out the prices of the cigarettes, often purchasing enough to fulfil her holiday break and beyond. The nicotine stick was expensive and pennies saved meant more to spend when on vacation. This time though, it was a special bottle of whisky that was on demand; a present to be given to the groom as a toast from Claire's daughter. She was unable to attend the upcoming wedding and had requested that her mother purchase a bottle to present to Mark on the eve of his impending nuptials.

The prices of alcohol were something unfamiliar to Jackie, a person who rarely drank anything of an alcoholic nature. Whisky wasn't a tipple she had ever really tried; deadening a toothache being the exception. Brandy and Babycham she recalled when courting her late husband, along with gin and orange, but never whisky. That was many moons ago, too many to count, and a weak cup of tea was her preference now. Jackie without a cup of tea when needed, would not be a good thing. A bear with a sore head came to mind.

Addictive as alcohol was, English breakfast tea was equally compulsive at times. Stranded on a deserted island without a cup of tea, to Jackie, was utterly unthinkable. Where would the world be without tea to drink? Breakfast tea it had to be, though. Jackie had tried Earl Grey once and had spat it out in disgust. Revolting to the extreme, the wealthy clientele could keep it, expensive as it was. Jackie had tried it, at least.

Claire decided on a bottle of whisky to suit and headed towards the check-out to purchase it. Once bought, a compulsory coffee was required whilst awaiting the signal to head to the appropriate gate for boarding; rather relax at a comfortable table in the departure lounge than walk directly to the gate needed.

Two latte coffees were enjoyed from the Costa Coffee establishment ahead of the impending flight. As things progressed, their plane was delayed by two hours. Par for the course where family holidays were concerned. What was new there? With a fourteen hour trip ahead of them, what was another two hours anyway?

They would arrive in Calgary at some point, that was for sure. It was a good job neither of them had a crystal ball. Claire's nerves wouldn't have taken it, for definite. Costa Coffee produced two more lattes each, whilst awaiting the extra time before boarding the plane, and more visits to the conveniences to offload the liquids drank.

Jackie, for one, had never feared a flight journey, although she probably should have. Due to having her lymph nodes removed from her right arm and around about the location, a tight compression sleeve was required for the flight duration. The threat of deep vein thrombosis, due to the absence of the lymph nodes had made it compulsory whenever she flew in an aeroplane. There were times, on short-haul trips, she'd forgotten and hastily put the sleeve on whilst in flight.

A visit to Egypt, a Nile cruise to be exact, had caused severe pain whilst wearing the contraption and her hand had turned blue and was very painful. Forced to lie down, taking up two seats (thankfully there were spare seats available on the flight), Jackie's head was dizzy throughout the entire flight. It should have put her off flying, and for others, it probably would have, but Jackie had so loved her travelling abroad, her holidays, and always put it to the back of her mind.

On returning to the UK, the hospital issued Jackie with a slightly bigger sleeve to wear in the future, one she has worn ever since without further repercussions. Lymph nodes or not, Claire's sister hadn't concerned herself about deep vein thrombosis. She'd already survived breast cancer and could survive anything else thrown at her, in her head that was. Her body might have different ideas in the future, but for now, the times ahead were promising.

The walk to the allocated gate appeared a long one and Jackie's walking stick helped her reach the number of the gate they'd required. The mandatory queue to board the plane was stood in, passports and boarding passes checked. Claire and Jackie were off on their travels yet again, and as Claire nervously sat down on the seat noted on the boarding pass, the doors closed and the pilot started the engine. There was no turning back now.

Chapter Three

The plane journey was managed easily enough for Jackie, her fears had never included travelling by air. Better to be blown up and know nothing, than drown in the water on a cruise liner, her philosophy. Jackie's mind did work overtime occasionally, well maybe more than occasionally. The time leading up to death itself would be so much longer in the water.

Added to that, Jackie's ability to swim had been hampered by an operation years ago; she could walk on the floor of a swimming pool, but as for actually swimming in the sea…images were nightmarish. Jackie had never spoken about such matters to her sister, ever.

Claire's fears hadn't just been flying-related. At sixty-plus years of age, she'd never partaken a cruise with John, or anyone else for that matter. Travelling great distances by coach, by car even, hadn't instilled great confidence either. A nervous traveller, she was happier on home ground and close to home. Nevertheless, she loved seeing new places and relished in regular sunshine holidays abroad. Purely out of necessity, Claire had done her utmost to put aside her fears and enjoy life.

That said, Jackie had managed several cruises in her lifetime herself, without thinking about anything too sinister. A week-long Nile cruise was probably one of her best, she'd recalled. A laid-back approach to a large cruise liner, and so relaxing and scenic. A beautiful memory, one spent with Alan, their daughter, and her young son (their grandson). At five years of age then, he was spoilt rotten by everyone there. A wonderful experience whilst recovering from illness, without any thoughts of drowning.

Claire had become anxious as the wheels left the ground, ultimately passing out in her seat. She was breathing, Jackie had checked, so left her to sleep as long as she was able to. It was a long flight, after all. The television, located on the back of the seat in front of her, was equipped with plenty of feature films, games and information regarding their journey forward. Jackie happily played the trivia games and quizzes before becoming bored.

Intellectually, the answers weren't connecting with her brain; her excuse anyway. Losing the game and having to start all over again was attempted way too many times for her liking, and it had become a tad tedious. It was time for a rest, a chance to rest her eyes. Admittedly, Jackie was never the brightest where quizzes were concerned.

Claire's and Jackie's youngest sister had been dealt with a high intellect whilst growing up, she recalled; Jackie's brain was merely average. Okay, in the context of things. We couldn't all be geniuses, could we?

Alan and Jackie's vacations alone usually included an attempt at a quiz in a local public house or taverna, or indeed a club house on a caravan site, wherever they were holidaying at the time. By the end of the week, their title name choice for their meagre attempt at answering the questions was usually "Always Last", and they were, most of the time. What did either of them know about the current trend in music and the names of the singers? General knowledge was a little better but not much.

It was time to give up for a while, Jackie decided. Claire was still asleep, sound. She wasn't snoring though, thankfully. Recalling Alan's snores, Jackie laughed to herself. Just imagining him being there in place of her sister had created a slight giggle; memories that would never fade. Jackie closed her eyes, relaxing her brain for a moment.

Food and liquid beverages had broken up the flight periodically, but it was still a long time to sit down. At home, Jackie could put the kettle on and make herself a cuppa whenever needed; she could have done with one right now, there and then. A mug full, rather than a tiny disposable cup that had hardly held any of the liquid at all. Two sips and the tea was gone!

Claire had woken up promptly, her ears hearing the trolley's arrival. Sitting upright, she'd eaten the meagre portion of food and drank her coffee. Now wide awake, the trivia games were given a go. Had she fared better than her sister? Jackie wasn't really watching, if she was honest. A five minute nap was attempted but given up almost immediately; sleep wasn't on her side, so back to Who Wants To Be A Millionaire it was.

The plane's descent had Claire flustered and she quietly closed her eyes in an attempt to shut it all out. It wasn't happening, the noise of the wheels touching land could never be classed as quiet; the bumps prominent as they drove the distance of the runway before coming to an abrupt halt. The plane appeared to rattle loudly along the ground, screeching noisily at first.

If they had been on a flight heading for Europe, namely Spain, Greece or Portugal (among others), a round of applause would have sounded throughout the plane, thanking the pilot for his or her exemplary job in getting them to their destination safely. This hadn't happened on the Canadian experience, but thankfully, the pilot reached the destined country without any difficulty at all. Well done, matey!

With the tickets regarding the connection from Toronto in Jackie's hand, the airport had now required indications to the checking desk in question. Where did they begin? The place was huge; queue after queue after queue of people, with and without luggage, heading for another destination. Their luggage would be transferred from the Gatwick plane to the Calgary one directly; they'd not be required to pick it up from the carousel. Something to be grateful for at least.

As they entered elevator after elevator, followed arrow after arrow, and walked and walked and walked, they finally found the check-in area needed. Promptly standing in the queue awaiting the next stage of their journey, all appeared good. Both sighed with relief, looking at each other and saying aloud together, 'What a trek.' Sisters they were, both thinking identically. They knew each other so well.

The Gatwick departure hadn't left on time, two hours late in fact, and consequently, as a result, their connection had been missed. Two bemused faces had asked the lady behind the desk what was to happen next. New and unknown territory, the girls were dumbstruck. A hotel voucher was given to them, vouchers for food that evening and breakfast the following morning. A shuttle bus outside would take them to the hotel and return them to the airport the next day.

A new flight was given to them for the afternoon of the following day. Phew! A day late in Calgary was better than not getting there at all. There were positives to every negative, supposedly.

'The taxi,' Claire suddenly remembered. 'I need to contact them and change it for tomorrow.' Lake Louise had been booked for four nights, too. An email was required, losing the first night there. One thing had led to another before getting to the destination wanted. A lapse in the connection from Toronto to Calgary broke the entire journey forward, upsetting the apple cart, so to speak.

Claire was promptly on the phone sorting things out on that score. Chester now had the time for the plane to land in Calgary the next day and promised to be there waiting for them. The sisters would hold their breaths in hope.

Jackie and Claire were now in Canada, and it was big and beautiful, just as Jackie had remembered it from years ago. Claire's first encounter with the country itself, a newfound experience was about to confront her. 'Hello, Canada,' Jackie whispered to herself. Was Alan with her? She so hoped he was there, in spirit. Putting a thumbs-up to the sky, Jackie was secretly hoping her late husband was watching over them. Somebody had to! A smile surfaced, finally.

Plans running smoothly never existed on vacations, she should have known that all too well. As they located the shuttle travelling to the hotel, after Claire had inhaled a more than urgent cigarette or two, surprises were at the ready, good or bad. Would the hotel replicate the one prior to the flight, near Gatwick airport, or be something amenable to both of them? Both held their breaths, crossed their fingers and hoped for the best.

Their prayers were answered, along with a shuttle bus full of other people who had missed their connection flight, too. Whether they had been on Jackie and Claire's flight from the UK wasn't known, and neither of them had asked the question. The hotel room was equipped with two double beds, a good-sized modern bathroom and a large watchable television.

A drawer housed sachets of tea, sugar, coffee and milk; the kettle stood proudly on the top of it, not far from the television and disposable cups were plentiful. A balcony enabled Jackie's sister to partake in her nicotine-based stick, all good there.

Now for some much-needed food. With tummies rumbling, they were seated in the dining room by a friendly staff member and quickly chose a meal from the menu, ordering coffee to drink. Finally, they relaxed, both shattered in mind and body. The hotel was of high class, clean and comfortable; they could easily have remained there as a paying guest for more than a single night.

That couldn't have been said for the previous accommodation.

Claire could have seen some of Toronto's favourites; the CN tower a must when there. The numerous shops and eateries, high-rise condominiums almost reaching to the sky. The local parks, are there to sit and relax; watching the black squirrels running around the grassy areas, sadly vermin to the Canadians, unwanted predators in the area.

Jackie recalled walking down Chinatown with Alan, a street lined with Chinese shops equipped with food, clothes and souvenirs. Every outlet showing China in its oriental style, whether food-based or otherwise. They spent ten days there, in Toronto, years back, and had loved the city. Climbing the CN tower, Alan lying full out on the glass floor that revealed the bottom of the building from a great height. Scary, but completely safe, staff had informed them. They had partaken in a coffee in the revolving restaurant there, taking in the fabulous views from above all around.

They had also visited Niagara Falls whilst there, revelling in the elated view from a helicopter ride above it; the maid of the mist voyage to the waterfall itself was an experience not imagined, ever. With the sprays from the water soaking every person on the boat, wearing a mandatory plastic macintosh given, was understood completely. A blind man on board delighted in the senses that the waterfall had given him, without even seeing the fall itself; his face told it all.

Casa Loma was a castle in Toronto, one that Jackie and Alan had paid a visit to whilst there. With an audio guide relating everything known about each and every room in the huge building and the extensive gardens, the hours spent there had well outweighed the entry cost. The décor itself and the well-tended gardens were to die for, all so beautifully cared for.

Alan had come up against problems, Jackie remembered; the audio guide was explaining another room to the one he was stood in on many occasions, entirely Alan's fault. He was never good, where anything of the gadget nature was concerned; par for the course, always.

Jackie recalled her time spent in Toronto with Alan. They loved the experience. Alan had so wanted to be spoilt and have his shoes shined by the street traders there, charging pennies really, to shine a gentleman's shoes enabling your face to be seen in them, almost. An ever-important facial grimace had crossed Alan's face as his shoes were expertly treated to a special experience, and one for Jackie's husband, for that matter. His expression was worth its weight in gold. Jackie could see his face there and then, just thinking about it.

Jackie's current eternity ring had been purchased in Toronto, the jewellery row of shops there. Jewellery outlet after jewellery outlet was checked out before buying Jackie's eternity ring, the one she still wears today. Her previous one had its day, literally, and was now discarded at home in her jewellery box, though probably should be thrown away, sentiments aside. Toronto had ticked all the boxes then, and the hotel that Jackie and Claire were sharing today hadn't disappointed either.

There was no time to explore the city as sisters, but who knew what could happen in the future? Bed was looming and hopefully, a good night's sleep was promised before beginning their journey again through Canada. Tomorrow's schedule was safely relayed in their heads, but as already discovered, things aren't always that clear-cut. Hoping plans would be straightforward in the morning, the lights were turned off and they both entered the land of nod, their bodies had needed sleep, so badly.

Chapter Four

Checking in at Toronto airport later the following morning had appeared easy enough at first. There was only the hand luggage to be scanned in the departure lounge; their suitcases being transferred internally. Claire's bottle of whisky had caused yet more issues, something entirely due to Gatwick's staff putting the posh bottle of alcohol in the wrong sealed bag.

Faced with a dilemma; either she purchased the bottle again at its full price or left the whisky behind. Claire decided to admit defeat and walk away. Needing to replace the alcoholic beverage at some stage during the vacation, she'd cussed inwardly but accepted the loss. Shrugging her shoulders, she wondered why everything had happened to her. Some staff couldn't be trusted, could they?

Others, those in Toronto airport supposedly would be supping the expensive drink and thanking an unknown traveller in the process; cheers and enjoy all!

The normal beverage was partaken, a Costa Coffee latte of course, whilst waiting to leave the airport for Calgary; drunk slowly and rather nervously by Jackie's sister, Claire. She did not want to embark on another aeroplane journey so soon after the previous one. A week or maybe two was usually a good space between the two. The day afterwards was far too soon, but necessary and unavoidable.

Lake Louise was yet another three and a half hours by taxi, once Calgary airport was reached, that was. The destination was getting closer but they weren't there yet, far from it. Canada was a huge expanse of country, big, bold and beautiful. With voids of nothing but fields and motorways, well, dual carriageways really, getting lost was easily managed. No issues there for the sisters! Jackie and Claire, and their respective partners…hmm.

They were experts at it and had been for a very long time. Unforeseen surprises were guaranteed, almost. Where Alan and John were concerned, getting to where they were going to was generally later rather than sooner, wherever they'd been heading, and how simple the navigational map had looked initially; UK or abroad, it hadn't mattered one iota.

The girls were on their own this time, only circumstances would discover whether their directions alone were better or worse than when with their other halves, their respective partners. A mystery in the making perhaps; a competitive streak, maybe. No, not really. Both of them would have preferred to have delighted in the journey, along with the regular known male company, epic as it was.

Alan was well out of the race through no fault of his own, but John would have been a welcome passenger, for sure. Where are you when we need you, John?

Boarding the plane, Claire's nerves were apparent but she bravely seated herself next to the window. Refusing to look out of the clear glass, she closed her eyes and anxiously waited for the engine to start. The plane began moving along the runway, heading for the skies above. She did not pass out this time, or slept for that matter, all good. Their journey on the huge bird in the sky was coming to its finale, until the adventure was over, that was.

Thankfully, the return journey would be so much easier; no connection to encounter. A direct flight from Calgary to Gatwick it was to be. A longer period flying, that said, but so much simpler and less nerve-racking; for Claire, anyway. Jackie had no fear of flying and had never been concerned about it, ever.

Travelling entailed a certain amount of risk, as life itself had. Any person who experienced a calm sailing throughout their entire lifetime, would, in Jackie's eyes, be unique and improbable, lying even. The trials and tribulations encountered from birth to adulthood would be devoid of a smooth ride, and whoever admitted to a life of tranquillity, would have come up with some hurdles somewhere along the road.

Things were never that simple, and, being honest with herself, the words dull and lifeless had come to mind. Adventures and catastrophes appealed so much more where words were concerned. Experiences in life were needed to expand one's character, whether good or bad occurrences, calm or terrifying. Where had Jackie and Claire ranked on that score? At the top of the list, probably!

A small plane with less seating, the Canadian connection from Toronto to Calgary was a little noisy in comparison to the flight out of the UK. Jackie had remembered catching a connecting flight from Los Angeles to Las Vegas with Alan, many moons ago. The plane was not dissimilar to a coach on wheels, with no frills flying and very noisy; bare metal floors and devoid of any curtains against the windows. It was a cold and cheap connection but had got them to their destination without any issues, surprisingly.

The hostess trolley, on Jackie and Claire's current flight, was wheeled back and forth, up and down the aisle, delivering refreshments of all sorts. Hot, cold, and alcoholic, the choice was endless. Tea and coffee were ordered, though probably three sips of tea or coffee were all the disposable cups held. Nevertheless, liquid replenishment it was, and all too welcome. A small meal was also delivered to each and every occupier of those taking up a seat on the plane; tempting their palates in readiness for when off the plane and on dry land.

For Claire, that time couldn't come soon enough. Three cheers for Jackie's sister's determination. Their younger brother had steadfastly refused to fly in an aeroplane, or any other form of airborne vehicle, for that matter. Holidays for him and his wife had to be taken in the UK, or not at all. No, it was, where he was concerned, and no it would always be. Maybe Michelle should join them on their next adventure; triple trouble could be even more exciting, who knew? Their next booked holiday, perhaps!

The plane landed and Jackie and Claire, after climbing down the metal stairs, followed the crowds towards passport control, continuing onto baggage reclaim. Luggage was strewn everywhere and a game of hunt for the correct suitcase began. Not centred around one particular area, baggage of all shapes and sizes, colours ranging from plain and drab to bright and luminous; old and new containers holding people's precious belongings, the sisters hadn't known exactly where to start.

What happened to the carousels evident in the majority of airports visited?

Jackie's suitcase was a run of the mill range, from one of the well-known establishments sold on the High Street. Black, soft cloth fabric, with two white stripes running through it. There was nothing that stood out against the mountain of luggage in front of them but she'd found her clothes carrier pretty quickly. The white cord dangling from the zip, there to differentiate it from identical suitcases, appeared to have done the trick. Now to find Claire's belongings.

They searched high and low, far and wide, and then double-checked the areas again (just in case). Her suitcase was a boring black, soft cloth fabric, but so much larger than Jackie's. Borrowed from her partner's mother, it had been big enough for two weeks, plus a few more days' vacation, and held wedding outfits and presents for the upcoming couple's big day.

Claire had tied a blue floral scarf around the handle to ease identification. The suitcase was nowhere to be seen. It just wasn't there. The needle in the haystack, Claire's belongings, just couldn't be found. It had disappeared into thin air. How could something so visible disappear, unless it hadn't been loaded onto the aeroplane in the first place? Jackie hadn't aired her thoughts to Claire on that score.

Reporting the loss to the human being sitting at the airport desk, they made their way to the exit, where the taxi driver had been patiently waiting for them. Everything was crossed that Claire would meet up with her suitcase sooner rather than later. What was it that they'd said about plain sailing from here on, a little earlier? It wasn't happening yet, anyway.

Chester, the very talkative driver, had them both educated very quickly on Canada and its history. Anything either of them wanted to know about their stay in the country, Chester was able to tell them; a mind of information on most topics, his head was a walking encyclopaedia, well almost! Keeping Jackie and Claire on their toes, alert and more importantly, awake; Chester was an inspiration with non-stop conversations. Most of it was interesting, they both agreed.

Three and a half hours of travelling to their first port of call, Lake Louise, the views outside of the windows were to die for, not that either had wanted to die, and a drive of more or less continuous dual carriageway, all the way there. The UK's motorways appeared so much more congested, the residents in a constant hurry to get to wherever they were going at the time.

Canadian drivers hadn't followed the same pattern, their driving was controlled with a more leisurely attitude. The Canadian maple leaf should have been given to the British drivers, for them to take a leaf out of their book. Miles and miles of road travelled without any signs of heated rush, tempers frayed, or accidents where patience had let its guard down. Heaven, or so it seemed.

Turning off the long straight road, indications in the form of road signs appeared at long last. Chester had still been talking away about one thing or another. He pointed to a residential area to the right of him, one almost built into the mountains and hills beyond, telling the sisters that it was where he resided with his wife and children. It looked stunning, and Jackie was envious. Completely up her street, she could happily live there. The lottery needed winning, fat chance there!

Both sisters turned off occasionally whilst he had carried on with his never-ending chitchat. Chester would prompt them with questions about the UK, forcing one of them to answer him, if they could. They'd not always known the answers, a walking encyclopaedia they weren't, and sadly, neither had entered university after high school had run its course.

Dumb they weren't, but a lot of life's history had bypassed them, that or else they'd not been interested in the subject to hand in the first place. The latter was probably the truth, for sure.

The views beyond had awoken them both completely, their senses now re-ignited after the long journey forward. Awe-inspiring and so beautiful, the mountains were in front of them now, almost calling to them. With the lakes in walking distance from the countryside beyond, it was truly a sight for sore eyes, and literally a painter's paradise. Stunning was another descriptive word recalled, one of many more somewhere in their heads.

A few hotels were now in sight, not situated close to each other; the distance between them expressing, as Jackie had surmised any roads, a retreat of sorts for all who had visited them. Claire's sister's excitement was euphoric; the kind of accommodation that was hers and Alan's idea of pure relaxation, with a chance to unwind from today's sometimes despairing world. Jackie's dream location, for sure, and they had still not reached their destination.

As Chester pulled up at a building with the name Deer Lodge written on the front of it, they couldn't quite believe their eyes, they'd gasped in pure delight. Was this where they were staying for three glorious days and nights?

'Is this it, Claire?' Jackie asked her sister. 'Is this where we are staying?' The excitement was evident in her facial expressions.

'Yes, Jackie. This is it. I take it you approve!' Claire spoke.

'Approved! It's definitely not Booking.com.' Ouch, she probably shouldn't have said that but couldn't help herself. The first accommodation had suddenly confronted her in her mind. 'We've not seen the inside yet, but…WOW.' She did not need to say anything else. Her face said it all; she'd definitely gone to heaven.

The sisters got out of the car, helped by Chester himself; he was a true gentleman as well as a more than capable driver. Time had suddenly stood still, just staring at the building in front of them. Neither sister moved for what had appeared to be ages. Chester's voice woke them up with a 'Well, shall we go inside?'

Jackie and Claire adhered to his request, walking into Deer Lodge with him, still in shock, totally transfixed. The adventures were about to begin, the first part, in any case.

Chapter Five

Chester helped unload their suitcases, well Jackie's anyway. Claire's was invisible sadly. The holdalls were carried by the girls, they weren't heavy but he had offered to take them from their hands, out of pure politeness. As they headed into the foyer of the lodge, it was Claire who checked them in. The lodge was as beautiful inside as it was outside; everything expected of a lodge and so much cosier than a hotel.

Character-wise, there was no comparison, in Jackie's eyes that was. Dark wood captured a log cabin effect, with the huge lounge fireplace equipped with logs to light the fire beneath it on a cold winter evening. Jackie had envisaged sitting there on the four-seater sofa, gazing at the lit fire and warming the cockles of her heart with Alan, whilst reading a paperback romantic novel in total oblivion. Relaxation in a nutshell! Something she had never actually done yet.

A large elk's head hung from the wall above it, quite eerie really, but in keeping with what was expected of a lodge, a log cabin even. There were other stuffed heads around too. Large portraits of people from times gone by were hung all around the walls of the lounge, their frames intricately crafted in the same dark wood, in keeping with the lodge's true character.

The atmosphere was cosy and unassuming, idyllic in fact. Both sisters were happy with their new location for the next three days and three nights. The smiles on their faces confirmed it, happy and contented looks had taken over the worried frowns from the day before. A tick in the box was noted by them both. All good on the Western front.

With their keys in hand, an indication as to where the rooms were located was signalled out to them by the receptionist. Jackie's sigh was apparent as two flights of stairs had been attempted, with luggage. Thankfully, an assistant was there to help, carrying the suitcase to the corridor where their home would be for the next few days. Somehow, they knew they would be treated like royalty, spoilt rotten. The advantages of a paying guest!

Without an elevator to levels above the ground floor, Jackie struggled, but not one to give in she would have got there in the end. Not a quitter, ever, Claire's sister wouldn't rest while there was breath in her lungs. With mobilities evident, a distorted body wasn't one without the ability to succeed. Looks weren't essential to mastering hurdles, and Jackie somehow managed most things, whether a pretty sight or not.

The rooms, one each, were in keeping with the lodge itself; small and adequate for their requirements whilst there. The en-suite bathroom housed a half-bath, shower over it, and the essential toilet and sink. Hanging space amounted to a small rail situated in an alcove of the room but more than adequate for their stay. Drawers to place clothing not requiring hanging up was enough, and a double bed with bedding in keeping with the lodge's character, was comfortable.

All clean and tidy, but there was something missing, something necessary; no kettle to make a morning cup of tea. Oh no! The British are renowned for their cups of tea, or coffee for some, on waking up from a night's shut-eye. Jackie had brought tea bags, dried milk and sweeteners with her in her suitcase; all in preparation for her early morning beverage.

Alan had been a stickler for his early morning cuppa on waking up, so much worse than Jackie on that score. A bear with a sore head he was, without the kettle boiling away in the room, on getting up after a night of slumber. A bear with a sore head...how relatable! Jackie laughed to herself just then; they were in Canada. A bear with a sore head, she'd tried to vision it and giggled to herself. What was she like?

A cup of tea was a must wherever they were on their holidays. Alan wasn't there in the Deer Lodge with her, or was he? A smile erupted from Jackie's face, certain that he was with her, though unseen. Telephoning the reception for a kettle to be sent up to her room, if possible, her prayers were indeed answered. Staff there quickly brought up two kettles, one each for the sisters. Assistance at its best.

Jackie could see the sigh of relief on Alan's face as if he'd been standing there, right next to her. Two cups were remembered too, vessels to drink the nectar of the Gods from. As regards Jackie settling herself into her room, for Claire, that was yet another story. On opening the door to her accommodation, one virtually identical to Jackie's, next door and in the same corridor; her holdall was the only thing requiring unpacking.

No suitcase to unload, and nothing heard én-route, whilst travelling in the taxi with Chester. Claire checked several times whilst travelling from Calgary to Lake Louise, whilst Chester was driving.

The location of her suitcase was still a mystery. The song, *It's a Mystery*, sung by Toyah Willcox, echoed in Jackie's head right then, for obvious reasons. A lovely song going way back and Claire's sister was suddenly singing it in her head. Careful not to voice the words out loud, in front of her sister, Jackie had silently giggled to herself. There was nothing funny about it, sadly so.

A suitcase's possessions were precious, she knew that only too well.

Very quickly, Jackie picked suitable clothing to give her sister from her own possessions, until the elusive clothes carrier had turned up. Thankful that they were of a similar size and height, their fashion trends were slightly different admittedly, but as needs must; beggars can't be choosers.

Claire was grateful for any form of help on the clothes front, until then.

The lake, Lake Louise, was a mere five minutes' walk from the lodge, even at Jackie's sometimes tortoise-like pace. A quick look around the outside of Deer Lodge itself had sufficed after arriving there exhausted. With their stomachs rumbling, food was on their minds, first and foremost. They could eat a horse, though not literally, as the saying goes, both sisters had needed feeding. The journey had been a long one, but the rewards…well, there were no words to describe the views in front of them. Wow, couldn't even justify it.

Canada was something else, for sure. Jackie felt privileged to be standing in front of the fantastic scenery all around them. No wonder there were so many paintings done of the landscape nearby. She was so looking forward to seeing

Lake Louise, in all its glory, the following morning. As Jackie's stomach rumbled, the dining room it was, to fill and sustain their hunger until the following day.

Homemade soup and warm crusty bread had sufficed, piping hot and super tasty and plenty of it, they'd not scraped on their portions. A single alcoholic drink complimented the meal, their eyes closing through sheer travelling exhaustion. It was time for bed, the day had been long and eventful, with the emphasis on eventful. Wherever Jackie and Claire were concerned, life could never ever be described as dull.

Occurrences out of the ordinary were something familiar in the family, throughout their childhood and beyond. With three other siblings, stories could be continuously told. Some good, some mediocre and others outright disastrous. The holiday focused on the two sisters though, and that's where it remained. Enough to contend with, without adding others into the equation.

Jackie and Claire's holiday bloopers were more than ample, memories to add to their long list of mishaps. Claire awoke first the next morning and ventured downstairs for a much-needed cigarette. Espying a small room off the lounge area, there for tea and coffee consumption, she prepared a cup of coffee and settled herself on one of the seats vacant to drink it. Already having drunk a coffee in her room, one was never enough for her; she always drank at least two cups before leaving for work in the morning.

The weather was gorgeous, the sun shining brightly through the windows. A cute little creature was running around the grass at a fast pace. It ventured nearer the window, in Claire's view, and stood up on its hind legs, so proudly and balancing well, peering into the lodge with its gaze directly at her. Not a meerkat, or a chipmunk, its behaviour was somewhat similar though. Cute and cuddly to look at, she'd discovered later after asking someone, that the creature was indeed a ground squirrel, sometimes referred to as a Gopher.

Looking around closer, there were several of them parading the lodge and running around after one another, reminiscent of children in play. Very amusing and therapeutic, as children always are. The grassy areas, particularly, appeared to be their favourite haunts. There were several photographs taken, a must. Smiling, Claire enjoyed her coffee before checking on Jackie. Was she awake now?

Jackie showered and dressed and was finishing off her cup of tea, as Claire knocked on the door. Breakfast wasn't included in the price of the lodge stay, but neither of them was hungry for food; lunch would be time enough to eat. Beverages alone had sufficed there. It was time for a walk and to discover their surroundings properly. It would have appeared rude not to! Picture-perfect it had looked, now to sample the goods, so to speak.

Mountain after mountain, tree after tree, grassy verges after fields with grass; awe-inspiring it all was. Eye-catching and magnificent, pretty wasn't a good enough description for what they were staring at, for sure. The photos continued to be captured along the way, each image so different and taken at an alternative angle. Budding photographers they weren't, but here, in Canada, they'd not needed to be of a professional standard.

Every photo was guaranteed to evoke interest, for certain. Conversation was at a minimum, both sisters taking in everything in sight; so much bigger and bolder than the scenery back home in the UK. More intense, more interesting, and much more in your face than England, Ireland, Scotland or Wales could ever match. Breathtaking as the scenery was there, back home, Canada had outdone it completely. The country was unique, no question about it.

The Fairmont Hotel had come into view as they crossed the road, a hotel only afforded by the wealthy to stay in, when on vacation. Completely out of Jackie or Claire's league, a night's accommodation there would probably be astronomical, price-wise. Posh was never Jackie's preference, just as well really. Working class the family were, and holidaying had amounted to familiar surroundings and similar holiday accommodation.

Gold-plated taps and over the top bathroom accessories were not something required by Jackie or Claire; a trouser press, who needed that? They were on holiday, rather than dressing up for a fancy dinner party. Jackie's worst nightmare! In all honesty, anything too posh would set Jackie's nerves on edge, and clean and tidy had well-outdone anything fancy and prestigious.

That was only Jackie's take on it, though; she did not include Claire's views on the subject. A half-bath, with a shower overhead, was fine. No complaints from either of them and definitely none from Claire's sister.

Crossing a small stream and a quaint stone bridge, they both stood still momentarily, completely hypnotised, transfixed in the moment. There, in front of them, in all its splendour, was the famous lake itself. Lake Louise looked glorious as they both walked further to the water's edge, with even more photos to take. Had they gone to heaven and not realised it?

Speechless, neither of them usually were, not generally. They were now, no words were spoken at all.

Focused solely on the view, the one that was directly in front of them, they couldn't remove their eyes for what appeared absolutely ages. They were fixated. Jackie suddenly thought about the men in their lives, their respective partners; late or otherwise.

Alan and John needed to be there, alongside the sisters, just to witness what they were actually seeing. Alan, from up above, could well be doing just that, but John was missing out, big time. Careers sometimes had gotten in the way of what really matters, and now, at this moment in time, it was Lake Louise that had taken precedence, centre stage, so to speak, for all the right reasons.

Jackie gazed upwards, towards the sky above. She also thanked Mark for inviting her to his wedding celebration in the very near future, quietly in her mind, that was. Without the invitation, she wouldn't be standing there now, at Lake Louise. There was a God, she was convinced, though she'd not always fully understood him completely.

Chapter Six

It was just a lake, Jackie reminded herself, as they both stood in front of it, completely transfixed. But it wasn't, it was Lake Louise, and they were in Canada, no less. Chew Valley Lake, near Bristol, was pretty. The lake incorporated in Llyn Llech Owain Country Park near Jackie's home was beautiful, relaxing and tranquil. A place holding treasured memories of walking around it with Alan and two of their grandsons.

Loch Ness, in Scotland, was enchanting and elusive; looking around its volume of water in the hope of finding the Loch Ness monster himself, or herself. Jackie wasn't sure whether the intrepid creature was of the male or female gender. Recalling a movie titled *Loch Ness*, starring Ted Danson as Dr Dempsey, an American scientist sent to Scotland to disprove the existence of the creature in the loch, Jackie had hoped that Nessie did exist.

Real or not, the lake was now a famous landmark in Scotland, and beautiful in the making.

It was on a tour of Scotland, a coach tour, that Alan and Jackie had encountered Loch Ness, and added two lifelong friends to their family. Lasting over twenty years, four had sadly now become two, but Mary and Jackie were still in touch and would remain so until their departure from this world. Visits and stays at each other's homes would continue, without question. The two men, namely Alan and Reginald, would always be missed from the foursome.

Lakes, in general, were there to unwind and totally relax. Sit awhile on a nearby seat and free people's minds from the everyday stress that living in itself involves. To gather one's thoughts and eradicate others, those not required. Positive mental attitude, the glory of the lakes had somehow helped free the bad, and leave the good thoughts; memories far too precious to forget. Jackie and Claire were there, at Lake Louise, and their feelings couldn't be described.

Powerful and hypnotic, it had somehow drawn them into the view that was so awe-inspiring; a sight for sore eyes if you like, all in a good way. Not the Bermuda Triangle, not similar at all. They'd not been sucked up into it, never to be seen again. They were both still there, in body and soul. The turquoise blue water somehow connected to the blue sky above, along with the sun in all its glory, shining down onto the water itself.

Completely clear and cloudless, the water held no signs of dirt or debris. Turquoise blue with various shades of other blues, the occasional white hue causing ripples of wonderful colours throughout the lake, from start to finish. Wow…beautiful couldn't really describe it. It was, as the saying goes…indescribable in its entirety.

Jackie would have loved to paint the picture on canvas…chance would be a fine thing. Her artistic talent was reminiscent of L. S. Lowry's painting, matchstick men impressive, not! She never won any prizes in school for her artwork, and wouldn't now, years later. Her grandsons had laughed at her attempt at drawing, her daughter in hysterics.

Not good in the context of things, for sure; rubbish with a capital "R".

Beyond the lake, the mountains stood, their heads held high. Some snow-covered peaks were evident in the hot humid weather in June. How high they actually were was written down somewhere. Claire and Jackie would find the information on a plaque or leaflet somewhere around, that was inevitable. A keepsake to show the family on their return home.

But the sisters were there in person, both stood there looking at the wonderment of a piece of history, a famous lake that they both realised had totally deserved its place in the history books.

A place visited by so many, and all for the right reasons. A fabulous creation born out of nature and not man-made. Jackie and Claire stood still, staring at the lake, for what had appeared ages. Photos had to be taken, from various different angles, that was mandatory. The procedure took maybe an hour or more, they weren't counting. Admiring the results afterwards would be well worth the time taken to study each and every photo. They'd not got to that stage yet.

Their phones were clicking away at every opportunity available. With visitors galore, avoiding people being included in the shots had increased the time creating the photos, but undeterred, they'd carried on with the task to hand. A wonderful experience causing no harm or undue pain. Slowly, slowly was the pace, but they had no time limit to contend with. The whole day was theirs for the taking. "Wow", they'd both uttered in unison, before repeating the word again, "Wow".

The weather on the day obviously drew different pictures of the lake, different scenarios, and Jackie had recalled the one day, six years back, she'd set eyes on Lake Louise for the very first time. Alan was there with her and they were celebrating their wedding anniversary, forty years of marriage. Had the image remembered then, mirrored the scenery Jackie and Claire were witnessing now? Absolutely not!

The rain hadn't stopped falling then, and the heavy clouds had hidden the mountains behind them completely. With the torrents of water descending from the sky continuously and very rapidly, causing a dark and dreary feel to the day, just keeping dry had been all-important. A mere few hours were spent dodging the rain, rather than studying the lake itself, in all its glory.

To be perfectly honest, both Jackie and Alan browsed around the inside of the Fairmont Hotel, rather than focusing on Lake Louise itself. Weather has a way of changing things; neither Jackie nor Alan had seen much of the lake then, the whole reason for the visit in the first place. Rain stopped playing, as it often does. Living in Wales, Jackie was more familiar than others where the temperamental weather was concerned. In Wales, it often rained in bucket loads!

The interior décor and elegance of the hotel received priority sadly. Elegance overload, no expense spared, the Fairmont Hotel had exceeded all expectations for those with expensive tastes, with a bank balance to match. Jackie was almost frightened to touch anything, for fear of damaging or dropping it. It would probably have cost their entire holiday monies just to replace it.

Not Jackie or Alan's preference, even if they could have afforded to stay or shop there. Much too posh, they'd decided. Alan hadn't liked posh, ever. The rain continued throughout their excursion to the famous lake, and a coach full of dripping wet visitors continued their journey without capturing the beauty and magnetism of the iconic lake.

Jackie and Claire were seeing it now though. A scene resplendent in every way, outdoing all seen before, impressive as it was at the time (and it was, all said and done) when glancing out of the windows of the coach, and then safely under cover and out of the pouring rain. Had the sisters gone to heaven? Obviously not, Alan wasn't there to greet them.

Jackie tapped Claire on the shoulder just then, indicating that a beverage was required back at Deer Lodge. Lake Louise was thirsty work, and this was still their first day. Amazing, absolutely amazing. Pinching herself hard, she let out an "Ouch" before confirming that today was actually real. Jackie, for one, was enjoying herself.

Alan and his wife spent two days in Banff on their fortieth wedding anniversary vacation, hence the excursion to Lake Louise. Banff wasn't that far away in the context of things, and a ride on the gondola, the cable car to the summit of the mountain, was something Claire had deserved to see for herself (with Jackie, of course). Claire wanted to take a dip in the hot springs in Banff; something neither Jackie nor Alan had been aware of whilst there at the time.

Being in Lake Louise, a regular bus service was within walking distance to various locations, Banff being one of them. Checking on the timetables, the sisters decided to venture there the next day, so Jackie had taken a photo of the times, there and back, for future reference. Seeing as much of the country in the short space of time they had there, Claire had her wits about her.

Plans were agreed on but Jackie's sister had forgotten one important issue. Her suitcase had still not been recovered, no word as to its whereabouts as yet. Jackie had packed just one bathing costume and they needed two to experience the hot springs, otherwise one of them would have missed out. Claire could have gone naked, another option!

There needed to be some clothes purchased in Banff beforehand, and a bathing costume for Claire was a priority, a must. A street fully equipped with retail outlets and eateries, they would definitely be heading in the right direction. They had to focus on the bears, though. Keep a sharp wit about them and an eager eye completely focused; only kidding, there was more chance of seeing one at Lake Louise than in the town of Banff. Never say never, as the saying goes.

They had actually seen one én-route to Lake Louise, Chester had pointed it out to them after spotting it whilst driving the motorway. Sat in a field, way out of reach, but completely visible. Who could miss it? Happy girls they were, but close enough as far as they were concerned. Neither had felt the impulse to want to smooth it.

Two lattes later sat comfortably in the lounge area of the lodge, both were totally relaxed. Cameras were glanced at quickly; they could scrutinise them more closely whilst in bed, safely tucked up for the night. Conversation amongst others there had been conducted casually, a hello or good morning often moved onto a more lengthy talk amongst strangers there.

All part of a holiday, they weren't alone in being there to see the splendour of Canada, wherever they were actually from in the world. People of all ages were there, in groups, couples, and some on their own, travelling solo.

Jackie had spoken to one particular gentleman, an American of similar age to both of the sisters. He'd not stated actually how old he was, and it would have been rude to ask the question. Ladies didn't do that, did they? As the conversation continued, it had transpired that he was there for a wedding celebration; the actual wedding had been conducted the day before. Had Jackie and Claire arrived at Deer Lodge the day before, their original arrival date, then, in all probability they could have witnessed the occasion.

Plans became delayed, through no fault of their own, so that hadn't happened. It would have been nice, Jackie had expressed to the gentleman in question. He was the father of the bride and had spoken highly of the lodge and the celebration itself. The location was absolutely stunning, who wouldn't want to get married there?

It would have been Jackie's dream, for sure. Preferential to the Fairmont Hotel, but that was only her opinion; others may decide differently and often did. What did Jackie know? A mere spectrum on a huge planet called Earth, she'd eaten up the landscape around her, revelling in the beauty of her surroundings. Beyond brilliant, Jackie had felt lucky to be alive.

Whilst holidaying in Las Vegas, years back, Jackie had recalled Alan wanting to renew their vows there. Something completely out of the blue, he expressed a wish to conduct the nuptials whilst vacating there. Jackie had refused, not wanting to go through a marriage ceremony again, they'd already done that and got the t-shirt, as the saying goes.

Now, if he'd asked the same question in Lake Louise, in hindsight, she would probably have replied positively. Las Vegas was unique in its way, as was Lake Louise, but Jackie had been under no illusion as to which she'd preferred, for a renewal of wedding vows, any roads. Forty-three years of marriage they had managed, and Jackie's negative response hadn't upset any apple carts.

Knowing how much Alan loved her, had brought happy tears to her eyes suddenly. Turning away from the gentleman, she reached for a handkerchief in her bag and pretended to wipe her nose.

An evening meal had been eaten in the lodge that night, with absolutely nothing to complain about. An alcoholic beverage and a large latte had sufficed until the following morning. Lake Louise had ticked all the boxes, imaginary ones, and they could visit it again tomorrow; she was on their doorstep calling them, with her elegance and charm. Who could refuse her? Definitely not the two sisters, Jackie and Claire.

'Roll on tomorrow,' they'd both said as they entered their rooms for the night. 'Sleep tight. Don't let the bedbugs bite,' they'd said in unison, smiling.

Chapter Seven

Getting to the bus stop the next morning, the weather was good; slightly cooler than the day before, but it was quite early in the morning and the sun still had its hat on, hiding some of the sunshine. Both sisters had dressed for the occasion, and Jackie carried a small bag containing her bathing costume and a beach towel. The thought of others seeing her in a bikini caused a frown on her face, not nice to see. Her views entirely, but a constantly protruding belly wasn't a pretty sight, it had required hiding for definite, so a bathing costume it was.

If Claire could purchase something similar along the way, the hot springs were on the to-do list for the day. Two excited teenagers, only kidding, but they'd felt younger than their actual years, were on their travels again. Today was indeed, another day. Another day to explore what Canada had to offer and they were so looking forward to the adventure ahead of them.

The bus journey was scenic, igniting happy thoughts along the way; what a wonderful place to live. Jackie, for one, was a little envious, maybe more than a little. The mountains were everywhere, green fields and small rivers, along with a few lakes being passed by along the way. Residential areas were uncovered, with retail outlets coming into view before disappearing altogether, out of sight.

Miles of landscape after landscape, all too beautiful to miss. To take one's eyes away would be such a waste, not that either of them had wanted to, that was.

Suddenly, the bus pulled into Banff and gasps were let out from both sisters' mouths. The scenery was absolutely astounding, unbelievably stunning. A road laden with shops, one after the other; food eatery after food eatery and more, much more. Staring them both in their faces, directly in front of them, were the mountains; heads higher than ones seen on their travels a few days earlier.

Flabbergasted, the phones were clicking away as they stepped from the bus to the pavement. A beautiful illusion, too precious not to capture. But it wasn't an illusion, it was real; a street lined with shop after shop after shop, with ginormous mountains stood proudly at the end of it. Words couldn't describe it properly, a photo had been required, compulsory vision.

The UK had nothing like it, as fascinating as some parts of the country were. Canada had beaten it, hands down. Stunning to the extreme, Banff was indeed jaw droppingly gorgeous. No doubt about it.

Jackie's memory of the two days she'd spent there with Alan had recalled the actual hotel they had stayed in. There it was, staring at her, opposite the bus stop. A huge smile engulfed Jackie's face as she took a photo of it, letting her sister know that she was familiar with the area. The memories recalled had put them both on the right track. Jackie's skin glowed through pure excitement. Alan's invisible body stood beside her, reliving the wonderful memories of years gone by.

It was time to go shopping, they both expressed. Banff, here we come!

The bear spray was still sold in most of the shops, there displayed in the windows for all to see. Jackie's mind asked the question, 'Could she stand in front of a bear and spray the contents over it?' 'No,' had been her reply, 'Not in a million years.'

Instinct would have told her to run as quickly as she could. That would have been a tall order for Claire's sister, as at times, just walking alone was painfully slow. Jackie would have been caught and gobbled up by the huge animal, the grizzly bear, without question. She'd have stood no chance, none whatsoever. A picture of herself being captured by a bear sent her into a trance until Claire tapped her on the shoulder to move onto the next shop.

Bear spray, did Jackie need to purchase a bottle? Conversation about the elusive spray had strangers, residents of Canada, enlighten them about the sticky substance in the bottle of spray. If needs must, the contents were used. A precautionary measure on hand for some; fishermen, avid walkers and the like. The chances of a bear walking down Banff's High Street, its main shopping area, were pretty remote. Too many people about probably, but never say never.

Jackie and Alan had witnessed a mother bear walking across a main road when visiting Canada last. The coach had stopped when a lady on it espied a baby bear in the trees, but sadly, it had disappeared soon afterwards. Shrieks from another lady had told them that the adult bear was behind the coach, walking across the road, without a care in the world it had seemed.

All had seen it but photos of the rare encounter were unable to be snapped quickly enough. The moment was seen but not captured. A tick on Jackie's bucket list, she was well chuffed at the time. Something not expected by anyone on the coach, or indeed the coach driver himself. Hysteria overload, well not quite, but an awesome experience nevertheless.

Recalling both of them, Alan and Jackie, taking a long walk through the woods, so to speak, with the waterfall and river in clear view alongside them; maybe they should have invested in the bear spray then. They'd not thought about it at the time. Thankfully, Jackie was still here to tell the tale.

If you go down in the woods today, you're sure of a big surprise. If you go down in the woods today, you'd better go in disguise. For every bear that ever there was, will gather there for certain because…The Teddy Bears Picnic song had suddenly come to mind, for why?

Jackie had no clue.

Claire managed to purchase a few clothing items, including a bathing costume. Prices were high, extortionate in Jackie's eyes, but necessary she'd fully realised. Being a thrifty person, morals wouldn't have allowed her to pay the price on the tags, but in this instance, Claire's sister would have bought, though begrudgingly.

Back at home, Jackie would have purchased two or three items for the price of one in Banff. With clothing a definite requirement for Claire; shorts, a t-shirt and a bathing costume, the receipts were kept safe to hopefully be refunded at a later date by the airline or via the insurance policy. Claire hoped her suitcase would be found soon, the sooner the better. Her bank balance would be heavily reduced otherwise, if not non-existent.

She'd cussed inwardly about something unimportant, usually. Damned suitcase, why did it have to go astray?

It had been time for a spot of lunch, but where to go? The eateries were there in abundance, so many to choose from, far too many; steak restaurants, Indian and Chinese choices, fish eateries and the normal burger bars. The list was endless and with people walking the street continuously, empty tables had to be looked for, too.

Finally seated in an upstairs restaurant, with views over the mountains on the doorstep, chicken was chosen by both girls, with coffee to quench their thirst. An alcoholic beverage could be on the agenda with the meal later, they'd both stated to the waiter. Jackie and Claire were on holiday after all. A time to let the boat out and why not? Normal day-to-day drinking was allowed to veer off the radar this time.

The meal was huge, a large plate full of chicken, fries and sweetcorn; savoury dips complimented the meal, tasty to the extreme. Definitely moreish, both girls' conversation stopped abruptly on given their food. There was eating to be done and they'd not realised just how hungry they were. Canadian meals were on a par with American appetites and Jackie should have realised that. One meal a day, she and Alan had eaten whilst there; the portions were ginormous in Banff anyway.

The weather was gorgeous sunshine and hot, just what the doctor had ordered. Not a cloud in the sky to be seen, all good there. Banff Hot Springs was next on the list, so perfect timing. A pool of water, fresh from the mountain springs. Their bodies deserved it, their excuse. A treat was called for whilst away, maybe more than one. Would they be revisiting Banff again? The odds were stacked against it.

Jackie stuck to water in the end, after her coffee, and so had Claire. Their bellies were well and truly expanding after the meal, not all eaten. Their eyes were bigger than their bellies, though not literally. Enough was enough and alcohol wouldn't have been a good idea, maybe later back in the Deer Lodge. On the food list, a small meal would be more than ample then, if actually needed at all.

Fear of sinking to the bottom of the pool, the hot springs, had registered on the sisters' brains then. 'Oh well,' they'd said. The visit was still happening, a once in a lifetime occurrence it was.

Going back to the UK, the size of a house was something neither of them had wanted. Short and dumpy, had raised an alarm, not a good look. Who could constantly eat portions of Banff's plate full of food? Jackie knew and had laughed. John could have, for sure. A tall, solid specimen of a man, he needed sustenance to survive, lots of it. He would have relished in eating the monstrous meal of meat until his belly was full. Lovely Jubbly, as Del Boy from Only Fools and Horses fame used to say!

They'd needed the walk to the hot springs, not that it was that far away really. With bellies full, the food required some movement throughout their bodies until they reached their destination. Swimming wasn't essential, relaxing being the operative word, the key, after all. As they entered the changing rooms there to change into their bathing costumes, Jackie dared not look at her figure in the full-length mirror. She did not want to see herself.

There were worse figures around, she knew, but confidence aside, her body wasn't hour glass, far from it. Lots of lumps and bumps along the way, she'd tried her best to lose weight, but it just wouldn't budge. Repulsive she wasn't, but a nicer shape to her 5ft 1in build would have been nice, and well appreciated. She wasn't obese, but at times felt like she was. It wasn't to be though, more is the pity.

The water was hot, 40 degrees hot and crystal clear. Heaven almost, and the girls loved it. With the sun shining down from the sky above that was heating the water up even more, eureka had to be the only word to describe the experience. Too hot at times, something quite alien to them where water temperature in their own baths at home was concerned.

From experience, Jackie would get into a steaming hot bath, so hot that her body would redden with the heat from it. Claire's bathing experience was similar, the hotter the better, and Amelia, their mother, had been just the same. An inheritance from her the girls had echoed in the hot springs, Amelia would have been in her element there. Her smile would have been huge, lapping it all up.

Thoughts of the slimly built lady of latter years, bathing alongside them, had both of them laughing. Luxury to the extreme, Amelia would lay in the hot sun for hours and hours, drinking up the moisture from its rays. Jackie, for one, would have fried, been burnt to a crisp, she'd known. Her skin would resemble a road map, with colours ranging from white, red and brown; along with peeling skin from body areas exposed most to the yellow sun high up in the sky.

Amelia, on holidays abroad, would be mistaken for a native of the country; the mother of the family in her older years. Brown and browner, the sun had worked its magic on her; something the girls hadn't inherited, for sure. A lobster,

Jackie would resemble, though Claire's pigment after the sun had reached it, was a good colour and an even tan.

Water, for Amelia, was an aphrodisiac. The huge waves in the sea would call to her and she wanted to be there, riding along with them even though she couldn't swim. Recalling the high waves in Greece, one year, a visit to celebrate Jackie's son's wedding; her son had lifted a frail grandmother into the water to enable her to relish in the glory of the sea and its roaring waves heading towards the seashore. She'd loved it, the exhilaration of it showing throughout her whole body. A child in an older lady's body, perhaps.

The hot springs would have exhaled the same excitement, they both knew, and they wished their mother there to experience and witness their time there. Sadly, Amelia had passed away years beforehand, but memories cannot be eradicated. Their mother's passion for rolling waves, hot water and sunshine was something neither of them would forget, ever.

Sat dangling their feet in the pool of hot liquid, with the sun's rays tanning their bodies, and overlooking the mountain almost reaching to the sky, who could want for more? Jackie and Claire delighted in what was an awe-inspiring picture, one not to be missed or taken for granted. Their bodies felt replenished, soft and silky, with minds so relaxed.

The moment mattered, but nothing else. Life's trivialities had been put aside for a few moments of pampering, something Jackie wasn't used to. Was she happy to be there? Absolutely, and Claire felt the same. Just for a while, life in general hadn't been given a thought. The two girls got the cream, and they were lapping it up!

Chapter Eight

From being laid-back and almost horizontal, the sisters proceeded to walk the short journey from the Banff hot springs to the gondola station, where the famous cable car would take them to the summit. A view, even more eye-catching, of Canada from way up high; the top of the tallest mountain, it had appeared no less. Were they in for a treat?

Jackie knew that they were as she'd ventured the gondola once beforehand, years back with Alan in tow. Claire's fear of everything travel related, well almost, had included such things as cable cars and elevators.

Their mother, Amelia, had absolutely hated elevators (or lifts as they were also known) until she had moved into a high-rise apartment block in her later years. Being on the sixth floor, she had no option but to take a ride in them. The fear was still there but needs must, and she had persevered whilst living in the apartment.

The alternative was to climb six flights of stairs daily, or whenever she ventured outside of the apartment. An elderly person with limited mobility issues at the end, the stairs were not even contemplated. The elevator it was, and she had gotten used to it, eventually. Claire handled it okay, too. Visiting her mother frequently, it was the best and quickest way to get to Amelia's front door. Brave, Claire was, and obstacles were beaten, cautiously. Nothing usually foxed her, not Jackie's sister.

The occupants of the elevator, throughout the day, had been a talking point, when either Jackie or Claire, or both, were visiting. Something sorely missed when Amelia made her final move to a one-bedroomed ground floor flat outside of the locality as her health declined. Neither sisters had realised the importance of a mere camera, one inserted into the elevator as a security device; one that had laughable connotations amongst the residents there, and one their mother was addicted to.

With the camera built into every television set of residents living in the building, enabling Amelia to view the whereabouts of the apartment occupants on a twenty-four hourly basis, her television was hardly used to watch actual programmes on it. Inspector Amelia could inform both sisters, when there, who was in the elevator and what apartment they had resided in, along with the floor of the apartment itself.

Espionage at its best, and, as they had both discovered, very addictive! The vain residents would check on their appearance, brush their hair and correct their make-up. Others would represent a drunken stupor, carrying cans of alcohol ready to get even more inebriated at home. Couples would be seen kissing, shouting (though the actual argument couldn't be heard) or standing still and silent.

Families had congregated in the elevator, loaded with groceries and household requirements.

Others had lovingly held their grandchildren's hands as they were lifted up to the appropriate floor. Wheelchairs pushed in and out of the elevator by relatives or carers of the occupant, those unable to walk too far, or indeed not at all. Amelia could recite their names to Jackie and Claire, she knew them all, by sight anyway.

When their mother was moved to a more mobility-safe area, with an apartment on the ground floor, they missed the activities shown on the camera. There was nothing to watch, all so boring. People's antics on a day-to-day basis were hysterical at times and in today's terms, the viewing was similar to gogglebox. A laugh a minute or sighs of amazement in the residents' characters. What were they thinking at the time?

They both paid the fare required to mount the gondola, and Claire's nerves were getting the better of her, yet again. The hefty entrance fee hadn't been something you could just walk away from, once purchased. Claire followed Jackie albeit reluctantly and they'd both stood in the queue in preparation to board the cable car to the summit of the mountain, the highest they had seen since setting foot in Canada.

With its clear glass virtually all around the gondola itself, Claire had sat down on a seat very quickly, almost immediately. As the cable car had moved from the ground into the air, Claire's nervousness was noticeable, so Jackie sat next to her; admiring the view, but keeping a close eye on her sibling. Jackie was the eldest, so that was her job, wasn't it?

As they moved upwards, travelling at speed through very tall tree after very tall tree, paths of greenery showing through them; the view looking downwards was stunning and Jackie caught sight of people walking through the forest of greenery. Were there any bears in there, she'd wondered.

Forests were filled with wildlife, whether they were mere insects, animals or snakes. Snakes…Jackie's fear suddenly overtook her brain, now in turmoil. She'd never been bitten by one, or come close up to one (except in the zoo behind barriers), but even watching a video or television programme relating to the world of snakes, frightened her to the extreme. She wouldn't be entering any forest in the near future; probably never if she'd anything to do with it.

The ride continued and the Fairmont Hotel had come into sight. The building was huge, with its width and depth of equal proportions, it had appeared anyway. From the air, the hotel stood on grounds equivalent to a row of terraced houses; so many residents could have lived there, Jackie's thoughts on it.

With Lake Louise evident alongside the hotel itself, the views were spectacular from high above. A picture-perfect moment to capture. How the rich lived, so differently to the likes of the working class. Nevertheless, it was worth seeing, well worth it. How the other half live! Maybe more than half. Jackie wasn't sure of the actual percentage and hadn't needed to know.

Buckingham Palace, the Queen's residence, now the King's, wouldn't have looked too dissimilar from the air; elegance and superiority shown from a mere cable car, the gondola, signalling what the two sisters were missing. Jackie, for one, wouldn't have swapped places with the rich (well, perhaps for a day to satisfy her curiosity); if she'd inherited a fortune, she would still shop at Poundland! You couldn't break the mould, not where Claire's sister was concerned.

A bump was felt, followed by the cable car stopping to an abrupt halt. An assistant opened the door, allowing Jackie and

Claire to disembark. Jackie's sister had survived the journey without too much fear; whether she'd closed her eyes to the scenery below, or had actually seen the sights, she did not ask. They were there, at the top, with time to experience Canada from above. A sight for sore eyes, in a truly good sense.

Their phones were removed from their bags, in readiness for the unseen images waiting to be captured. There had to be a few, hadn't there? As they walked around the perimeter of the path, a circular one that extended the views around 360 degrees of beautiful scenery, neither of them knew where to start, or where to finish for that matter.

Visitors in abundance walked the path several times, clicking constantly on cameras and mobile phones. Selfies were taken, with the background including the views from above; a perfect picture to take back home with them, evidence of reaching the summit; proof that they were there to witness everything around in all its glory. Breathtakingly beautiful in its entirety.

A full scale model of a bear was the centre of attention at one point; a chance for Jackie and Claire to have a photo taken next to it, individually. The silver statue stood tall, a model there for visitors to enjoy. The bear was a big part of Canada's history, after all. Jackie's initial attempt to capture the bear failed miserably, the head had been decapitated. Oh no, it had required another take!

People from all walks of life, from all parts of the world, were there in droves, to experience the beauty of the country, relatively new in the history book. From the Japanese, Chinese, and people from further afield, to Americans and the British. All had come to see what Canada had to offer, and so far nothing had disappointed. It was early days, the sisters knew, but so far so good.

Were the girls' luck about to change for the better? Things looked promising, and the weather was gorgeous sunshine, all good. Things were looking rosy for a change. No mishaps or unforeseen events, as yet. A day of memories for the future without anything sinister occurring, but the day hadn't ended, it was still daylight. Luck had a habit of turning for the worst, they both knew all too well.

Claire's suitcase still hadn't been found, but on a positive note, there'd been plenty of time for it to make an appearance, hadn't there? For now, the clothes container had been temporarily forgotten, in favour of what they were experiencing now, the moment. Pure heaven in itself, Canada was ticking all the boxes.

Their journey had only just begun, everything looking positive. There was so much more to come, more areas of the huge country to devour and explore; they'd only just started. The coffee shop had needed a visit, and two large lattes and two giant chocolate chip cookies were purchased.

They sat outside to eat them and replenish their thirst, a priority.

An evening meal back at Deer Lodge had been the plan, not that either of them were hungry; their lunch in Banff had been of a substantial amount and they had not really needed the cookies. They had looked too nice to resist. Alan and John would have done similar and bought them just because they were there. John wouldn't have allowed them to sit there on the shelf, no way!

The souvenir shop was a must, there to browse and deliberate as to whether to splash out on a momentum of the summit, or a present to take back to family members. Nothing had taken their eye, and prices weren't cheap, only to be expected really. There had to be a dollar shop somewhere on route for souvenirs and they'd plenty of time to buy trinkets, of sorts. More ornaments to add to the too many already back home, but visitors still bought, it was mandatory.

Heading back towards the cable car, going downwards this time, Claire appeared relatively calm. To Jackie, the ride back down was more exhilarating than the reverse. She seated herself facing the drop downhill, so maybe that was why. Whatever, she wasn't disappointed and yet more photos were taken until they'd reached the bottom; with yet another bump, one expected this time.

The bus back home, to Deer Lodge, was taken quietly. Two sisters had managed a fun-filled day easily enough, with no mishaps. How did that happen? Both were ready for an early night, once back at Lake Louise, there'd been no complaints from either of them. Smiles adorned their faces. Life was good, very good.

A small snack and an alcoholic drink, white wine for Jackie, had finished the day off nicely. It had been time for bed, quite early really, but they had managed to put a lot into the whole day. Jackie's legs and stomach had surpassed her usual exercise, and a short visit to the hot tub in the lodge when reaching their accommodation, much later in the afternoon, had all but done her in.

They had to sample the hot tub at the top of the lodge, it was compulsory. Another 40 degree dip in a much smaller pool, so to speak. The sun was still shining brightly and the views from the top of the building had both girls gasping for breath. It was amazing, and truly worth the effort to climb the stairs to the top of the lodge. A day of getting wet, dry and then wet again.

As they'd entered their rooms to prepare for their evening meal, yet another wet experience had occurred, a shower! Jackie hadn't complained but her body was ready to give up. She needed to be laid horizontally in bed, resting parts of her anatomy in preparation for the following day. Another day in Lake Louise, then they would be off on their travels again. The next destination was to be Edmonton, for a whole week.

Chapter Nine

Jackie awoke quite early the next morning, deciding to have a hot bath in the half-sized one there. She'd plenty of time and the bath was a definite advantage for the "shorties" of this world. John wouldn't have looked a pretty sight in it, being over six feet in height. She laughed just thinking about it, imagining him sitting in it, his knees bent unable to straighten them. The water wouldn't have reached the parts needing washing, for sure.

A silent chuckle crossed her face. She was thoroughly immersed in Canada and the sisterly journey they were encountering. Happy as Larry, as the saying goes, but Jackie had no idea who Larry was! Whoever he was, Claire's sister was on a par with him. Life had suddenly become exciting. Maybe only for a while, a little while, but beggars couldn't be choosers. There she was, off again with the sayings of old, but how true they were, she'd realised.

A nice soak to relax her stiff bones, stomach and legs was called for, and the water was piping hot, just what the doctor had ordered. She washed her body and hair before relaxing in the bath for what had seemed ages, and probably was; her mind was devoid of anything negative, all memorable and pleasurable experiences. Completely calm and contented,

Jackie was. She lapped up the tranquil time to herself, just doing nothing.

It hadn't taken much to satisfy her, not as a rule. Dressing slowly, after making the bed, she picked up her bag and headed out of the room. A cup of tea downstairs, gazing out onto the lodge's outdoors, was her intention. Cups of tea were endless, but essential, where Jackie was concerned. Claire could still be asleep, so she did not knock on her door. They would find each other easily enough, somewhere around.

Heading towards the small room of the lounge, where tea and coffee were available, she stopped abruptly. The room was closed, cordoned off with tape, and the dispensers along with the tea and coffee supplies, were situated in the lounge area itself. Jackie hadn't thought too much regarding the reason and made herself a cup of tea. She was sitting on one of the comfortable seats admiring the view from the window, something she knew she would never tire of when Claire walked through the side door and entered the lounge.

Likewise, Claire woke early and went for a walk around the lake. Helping herself to a coffee, her preference, she'd seated herself opposite Jackie and conversation between the two of them had begun. There had been a leak in the ceiling of the small room next to the lounge, hence it being temporarily closed to residents, Claire had informed Jackie. 'Oh,' Jackie had said.

Things did happen and neither of them had thought any more on the subject. Provisions had been put into place to continue the beverage supplements, and supposedly, the leak would be sorted out soon. The Deer Lodge wasn't about to close its doors to residents because of the dilemma and there would always be a back-up plan in place. Businesses had relied upon it and daily life continued without too much hindrance.

They decided on another bus journey, a small one this time, much smaller than Banff. A retail outlet, of sorts, had been passed when Chester dropped them off at Deer Lodge; a chance to maybe purchase more clothing items for Claire, for starters. As they both walked towards the bus stop, a new day of discovery was about to be embarked upon. Shopping was fun whilst on holiday, not in the same league as home when purchasing everyday necessities; boring, oh so boring.

There appeared to be plenty of outlets, more than enough for the sisters. Espying a "booze" store there, selling every alcoholic drink known to man, though not to Jackie; Claire's knowledge on the drinks front was far more superior to her sister's. That wasn't to say that Jackie hadn't drunk her fair share of alcohol as a teenager though, she had. Palates change over the years, and hers had, usually abstaining completely out of pure choice.

'Whisky,' Claire's voice had shouted loudly. 'I can get a bottle of whisky here.' They purchased a lot more than the bottle of whisky. Jackie's buy amounted to miniature bottles to take home for presents, though nothing for herself. She no longer stashed bottles in a cabinet for Christmas and other occasions to celebrate. Since Alan's departure from this world, family visits to her home were almost non-existent. The parties had stopped play, forever.

Alan's voice on the karaoke machine, singing Elvis Presley songs galore, had the occasional change to Roy Orbison and Patsy Cline, Pretty Woman and Crazy being firm favourites there. The grandsons had held the microphone, attempting some noise in tune; hearing their voices echoing throughout the living room. Jackie had loved listening to them, trying to copy their granddad, but very badly. They'd tried so hard, wanting to imitate him.

Laughs throughout the room could be heard, all in good nature. The gorgeous little darlings were so infectious, so young and so innocent.

Did Jackie miss the get-togethers? Absolutely, yes, without a doubt. They were a reason to bring the family together, a break from day-to-day normality and catching up with one another. Illnesses and death were always a way of reuniting family members, but partying was much more enjoyable. Who wouldn't agree?

Silence is Golden, another hit song of the decade, the title wasn't always true. Silence was good for a while, as long as it hadn't been consistent or forever. Family was all-important, whether noisy or quiet. Jackie would have missed them all, for sure. Catastrophes aside, Jackie had known that their presence, however long or short, infrequent or regular, was a must to keep her sane.

In all honesty, Claire's sister couldn't have coped with being alone all day and every day. A break from normality was good, as long as it was just that, a break.

The other outlets were souvenir orientated, mainly. A few clothing accessories were seen there, very expensive and not suitable for Claire's requirements in any case. Jackie had picked up an animal back pack for one of her grandsons; he had a bang to the head in school that morning and a visit to the general practice to be checked out had occurred. Her daughter had sent a photo of the six year old feeling so sorry for himself. Poor thing, Jackie could have cried for him.

Was it the hospital her daughter had taken him to? Jackie's memory had suddenly taken a turn for the worse. Old age didn't do anyone any favours, her take on things. Forgetfulness, at times, was frustrating. She usually remembered after a long pause. Dementia hadn't set in, yet. Grandma's mind was playing up again and not for the first time!

There were a few eateries there, some to sit in and relax, others being take-away outlets. They'd chosen the take-away, after noticing a range of picnic tables and benches available at the rear of the shops. A river could be seen next to them, alongside most of the benches, and a bridge as far as they could tell. The weather was gorgeous; why sit inside when they could lap up the sunshine? Both sisters had totally agreed.

It had taken absolutely ages to get served, a lifetime it appeared. Hot coffees and pastries were purchased, along with to-die-for cakes, huge and irresistible. If they'd been watching their figures, then the diet would have been broken, without a doubt. They were on holiday and neither of them was conscious of their figures, nor cared for that matter. Fat and frumpy, skinny and lean, at their ages going with the flow was life. Eating was there to be savoured, whether healthy meals or indeed fattening, it didn't matter one iota.

John would have loved Claire if she resembled an oompa loompa; he was besotted with her. Jackie had no intention of finding a replacement for Alan. Her life had been content with him, all forty-five years of it. Life hadn't always panned out as hoped, and there were the inevitable arguments along the way, she wouldn't admit otherwise. Alan was no longer with her but he'd been enough for her lifespan and always would be.

Jackie's figure hadn't mattered to her, she'd not been out to impress anybody. An oompa loompa was okay for her too, not that Claire was one!

With their food choices purchased and packaged, they headed towards a vacant picnic bench to eat their lunch. There were more than a few available, those devoid of bums on seats. They decided on one overlooking the river and near the railway bridge. Watching a large train with carriages seemingly never-ending; carrying goods of all descriptions if the words written on the front of them were to be believed. The train sailed past the line at a very quick pace, a railway bridge obviously still used on a regular basis.

The picnic area was a welcome break from shopping, a laid-back place to relax and revel in the beauty of even more glorious scenery; one situated behind a shopping outlet and a complete surprise to both of them. The ground squirrels were out in force there to tempt those around to part with some of their purchased lunch. Who could resist the fascinating creatures standing upright on two feet, studying the people around them in detail?

Now where should they go? The choices were endless, those unwrapping cooked foods to feed their hungry bellies. Both Jackie and Claire had given in and fed them, laughing as they had hurried to the morsels of food on the ground before another ground squirrel had gotten to it first. Of course, the phones had come out again, clicking away at their mischievous antics and furious fight for food.

Who could dislike them? They weren't doing any harm, were they?

Sadly, the sisters weren't Canadians and were completely unaware of the scale of ground squirrels inhabiting the country. Foxes, in the UK, though pretty to look at, were considered a nuisance to the environment and many had been lost merely crossing the road. Motor vehicles had gotten in the way, they did not stand a chance. Maybe they should have studied the Highway Code.

Only kidding!

Time was taken to devour their food and take-away coffees, a welcome breather after browsing the shops. The times for the return journey on the bus had been noted, and they headed back to the bus stop with plenty of time to spare. Claire hadn't added to her wardrobe as yet, but she'd known, well informed really, that Edmonton was a city where clothing outlets would be in abundance; she could wait a few more days. Maybe her suitcase would be waiting for her at Deer Lodge on her return. She could hope, couldn't she?

There was no harm in dreaming, no harm at all. Disappointment raised its ugly head yet again. Claire's suitcase was still missing and no word via emails put any more light on its disappearance. The receptionist shook her head negatively when asked but then changed the subject completely. She wanted to know who had been occupying room number 206. Jackie had put her hand up. The number on her room key confirmed that the acknowledgement was indeed correct.

Apologising, the receptionist requested that Jackie change rooms and handed her the key to the one next door; a vacant and unoccupied space. They'd only one night left before departing the lodge in search of city life in a place called Edmonton, Mark and Louise's residential area. Jackie hadn't argued and was about to ask the question why when the lady behind the counter explained the reason behind the move.

Claire's sister had become red-faced, showing surprise and humiliation; she did not know which way to turn. The leak in the small room next to the lounge had appeared to be due to her. Jackie's room was directly above it. Gobsmacked, mortified, embarrassed, her facial grimace had shown it all. At the precise time of the leak, she'd been relaxing in the half-bath, she realised.

What had she done?

Reassurance from the receptionist told Jackie that the plumbing was ancient, antique, and renovations were to be implemented at the end of the year, including a brand new plumbing system. She hadn't flooded the lodge, well not on purpose in any case. Even with the explanation for the catastrophe, that's what it was, Jackie had felt a tad guilty. Why hadn't she just had a shower that morning?

Moving her belongings next door was no big deal. Claire had helped, and at the end of the day, it was just one more night, sadly. She could honestly say, hand on heart, that Lake Louise and the Deer Lodge were going to be missed. Once more, as per the sisters' regular course of action, things hadn't gone to plan. Jackie would be remembered for damaging a part of the building, without even realising it. What was going to happen next?

Chapter Ten

They still had a few hours to spare, after waking up the next morning, before Chester was due to pick them up, that was. Time for breakfast and another final look at the lake, until it was time to leave the location they both loved. Jackie was speaking for Claire, though she was certain, on this account, that the adoration of the area was reciprocated. She did not know her sister well enough if her presumption was indeed wrong.

They were about to encounter more of the Canadian territory though, a definite plus for the two sisters. Claire, since being in Canada, wanted to sample the pancakes and both ordered a plate full each that morning. Had their eyes been bigger than their bellies? It appeared so on this occasion, one portion for them both would have sufficed. Canadian meals at their best.

The pancakes, large and very thickly prepared, sat on their plates looking up at them before Jackie and Claire eventually tucked in, attempting to demolish the huge meal. A strawberry cream, elegantly piped into a flower shape had accompanied the pancakes, with maple syrup topping them off, not sparingly. The rivers of syrup were almost covering the entire pancakes. A heart attack waiting to happen, Jackie initially thought, the calories there had to be high, astronomical really.

It had been a treat for the sisters, a well-deserved one at that. They were on holiday and hadn't required an excuse. Where were the men when they needed them? Their appetites would have dwindled their plates of pancakes down, a little at any rate. Alan wouldn't have been able to help now, but John would have eaten some of the surplus, and there were going to be leftovers, they both knew.

Neither of them had cleared their plates, surprisingly. Their stomachs couldn't take in any more food. Bloated bellies were evident through their clothes; perhaps they should have dressed with different tops, ones that were looser. Hindsight was a wonderful thing! They couldn't do anything about it now and that much-needed final walk to Lake Louise would be more than beneficial, just to feel more comfortable again.

Two beached whales had come to mind, not nice! Claire's wishes had been granted. She'd received her pancake meal and devoured it, what she could eat, that was. Living like queens, both Jackie and Claire would have to come down to Earth at some point. Today wasn't the day, there was plenty more to come and perhaps another pancake meal to sample before returning to the UK. A smaller portion please, Jackie had secretly hoped for.

Their belongings were packed up; Jackie's suitcase and her hand luggage, along with Claire's holdall. The lovely male assistant carried Jackie's suitcase down the two flights of stairs to the reception area, and both handed in their keys, the ones belonging to their rooms. The walk to the lake left Jackie almost bereft.

She did not want to leave. The unshed tears in her eyes remained there, unshed. Claire hadn't noticed her sister's emotional state, thankfully. In another life, would Claire's sister like to have lived and worked at Lake Louise? Absolutely, she'd have been in her element. Needs aside, Jackie had a son and a daughter, and five grandsons. She adored them all, and that's where her loyalties lay.

Lake Louise was idyllic for others there, and for a holiday experience, awe-inspiring. Jackie had been oh so thankful. There was a God up there, she was convinced. Grateful for the few days there, both sisters waved goodbye to the famous lake with that secret ingredient. One where memories were made and wishes were granted.

Saying goodbye to the receptionists there was tearful; they both thanked each person individually for their help during their stay at Deer Lodge. Claire's suitcase had still not been found, but not for the want of trying; a mystery in the making. Chester loaded up his vehicle with the girls' belongings. On their travels again they were.

Their driver, Chester, was his usual self, talking non-stop about this, that and the other. The drive was going to be a long one again, three to four hours minimum. Another dual carriageway experience, travelling the busy road with ease. Chester was more than used to it; it was his job after all.

'Like riding a bicycle,' he mentioned when the girls had brought it into conversation, and Jackie laughed at the remark.

She'd never ever been able to ride a bicycle, despite several attempts as a child; her chances of mastering the busy dual carriageways in Canada were hopeless. It wasn't something she would have wanted to attempt though; at home, the motorway was similar to the Devil incarnate, frightening! Not an enjoyable experience but sometimes necessary to get to where Jackie had wanted to go. Jackie and driving, well, she'd have abstained if she could have.

Driving in the UK was done purely out of need, rather than choice. In reality, she'd hated it, but there'd been no other option for her. Alan was sorely missed for many reasons; driving her everywhere she couldn't, being just one of them. Her home was situated semi-rural, neither town nor countryside-based, and most things required meant driving to its destination. Jackie loved her home though, so a car was an essential requirement, and being able to drive.

Conversation had gone hand in hand, par for the course, for an expert like Chester. The weather hadn't changed, the sun was still shining; the temperature remained hot. Summer clothing continued to be worn, no need for jumpers and jackets. The sun was tanning their skins nicely, cooking their bodies slowly, and Chester commented on their colouring, noticing their glowing figures. Sunshine had so made a difference, sun-tanned was preferential to pale and dull, every day.

As they entered the area where, on the way there, Chester pointed out the huge bear sitting in the middle of the field. 'His territory,' their driver had said at the time. Was the bear there again for the girls to see? They were in luck, the animal was indeed there again, but so were crowds of people. All stopped and stood outside of the field, taking photos of the beast from a very close range.

'A big mistake,' Chester stated. The bear, as delightful as he had looked, could easily turn on them. As famous as the creature was, was it wise to make a spectacle of it? 'Continue driving,' their driver said. Safety first as always. People could be so ignorant, at times. Dangerous to the extreme, Chester had tutted to himself as he continued driving the girls to their destination.

There was a toilet stop for the girls, a chance to stretch their legs and for Claire to smoke a cigarette. Ten minutes break and off they were again, heading for Edmonton. The scenery hadn't changed, still as enchanting as it was on the way to Lake Louise. Miles and miles of greenery and mountains, with residential areas, passed along the way, all followed by yet more miles and miles of countryside.

Chester had pointed out Canmore again, a residential area set up in the mountains, with parts of it overlooking the dual carriageway. That was where their driver had lived with his wife and children, he'd stated. Both girls were envious and said so. Jackie's kitchen window overlooked a mountain and farmland, but Canada's residential properties outlook was far more superior. They were the lucky ones, even if they hadn't realised it themselves.

The UK couldn't compete on that score; whether the head counts were far too high, Jackie hadn't known. Geography had never been one of her strongest subjects in school, or later in life. A mind of useless knowledge was more to her liking, things picked up during conversation. Whether right or wrong, some information had stuck in her head, for no particular reason.

Both sisters have had various jobs since leaving school, neither of them out of work for very long. Apart from the gaps whilst caring for their young children, part-time and full-time jobs had ranged from shop work, insurance and cleaning jobs; waitressing, caring for the elderly and evening work in a fish and chip shop, to name just a few. If a salary was rewarded, they had mastered most things.

A Jack of all trades and master of none; a saying suiting them both admirably. They learnt a lot over the years, history and geography lessons picked up somewhere along the line by workers and customers known to them; knowledge in abundance, not really! Names of countries were familiar, but where on the globe they were, neither would have had a clue.

Chester continued to educate Jackie and Claire on Canada and its habits, amongst other things. Quizzing him on clothing outlets in Edmonton, he was a mind of information on the subject.

Girls loved their clothes, and the sisters were no exception there. Looking good was healthy for both mind and body alike. Had they stored the names of well-known outlets safely in their heads, though? Only time will tell.

Finally, and after a long journey, Chester pulled off the dual carriageway. They were heading for Edmonton at last, and the street signs were confirming it. Two excited females suddenly awoke from their journey, eager to get to their next destination. Claire had given Chester a postcode, the name of a street and a number of a house. It was up to him to find the location, the area and a part of the world that Mark and Louise resided in.

They both held their breaths, waiting patiently for the vehicle to come to a halt, and it did, finally. They were there and breathing was returned to normal, as the house had come into view. Neither of them knew what to expect, as Mark had rented the accommodation for them. It was their present for accepting the invitation to their wedding, knowing they were travelling a more than simple journey to get to them.

None of the girls had any input in the Edmonton house, a week-long break in another part of Canada. On the outside, it resembled a detached residence in an ordinary street back home. Nothing spectacular, but on the other hand, nothing drab or dismal either. A house in a tree-lined street, where people resided and worked; their home to bring up their children and do what everyone around had done, lived. Normal existence for everyone, one that Jackie and Claire were all too familiar with.

On opening the front door, after inputting a sequence of numbers into the combination lock attached to it; no key evident at all, very strange for both of them. A memory game they would both have to master for the entire week, for fear of being locked out of the house. Keys for Jackie could sometimes cause problems due to the arthritis in her fingers; doors couldn't be opened without asking another person to help. Embarrassing at times.

The combination lock was a blessing in disguise for her; she wouldn't be left with egg on her face.

The door opened into a large open-plan room, comprising of a lounge area, kitchen and dining area combined. A decent-sized living area with a large corner suite overlooked the large bay window, throwing plenty of light into the room. Stood on a large easel-type accessory was a huge television set, big enough to be seen throughout the entire room.

A bamboo cane coffee table with a thick clear glass top was parked central to the sofa and allowed plenty of room to move around it. Was it cosy? Well, not in Jackie's eyes. Cosy to her had included a fireplace and a fire of sorts; coal, electric or gas, it hadn't mattered which. A large carpet rug in front of it to create an ambience of a living space; somewhere to relax and unwind after a long day. A low lighting in the form of a table lamp would have set the scene perfectly, in Jackie's eyes that was.

The area in the house hadn't included this, but neither had a lot of residential premises back in the UK. Most of the newly built properties hadn't featured any fireplaces, only a central heating system throughout the house. It was a matter of choice, and people's preferences were never the same. Older properties were Claire's sister's favourites, but there was nothing wrong with what they were looking at now, nothing at all.

The kitchen area was huge and the appliances were even bigger. A fridge freezer that wouldn't have fitted into Jackie's kitchen back home, with enough room to fill a month's supply of fridge food, in her reckoning, anyway. The oven was of the double variation, not that any of them had wanted to be cooking the entire week; they were on holiday! Meals out and takeaways were more to their liking, but never say never. A day spent inside the house totally relaxing might happen, who knew? Tomorrow was another day.

There was a dishwasher, a washing machine and a tumble dryer. Plenty of storage around the worktop space and a larder-type cupboard, filled with everyday needs. Washing up liquid bottles galore, washing powder and dishwasher tablets; dishcloths, tea towels and bleach. Everything required for kitchen use and more. They wouldn't have to buy anything of that nature, for certain. A dining table and dresser had taken up one side of the kitchen, with six chairs around it.

A teak-coloured wood table with matching chairs, and the dresser matched it perfectly. A vase of artificial flowers was arranged on one of the shelves in the dresser, along with a few ornaments placed on other shelves. It made it look homely and not so sparse. A fruit bowl in clear glass had taken centre stage on the dining table, there to place any fruit purchased in.

The normal appliances were all there. A kettle, a toaster and a microwave; jars of t-bags, coffee (instant and ground) and a coffee percolator. Jackie had no clue how to use it, this was Claire's domain. It was all there, and both ladies were impressed. Home away from home, it appeared. All good on the Western front! They hadn't ventured up the stairs, yet!

Chapter Eleven

Claire was the first to climb the stairs and investigate the rest of the house. There were three large bedrooms, all housing a double bed and adequate bedroom furniture. One was devoid of a hanging wardrobe though, but the master bedroom had plenty of hanging space, more than enough to compensate for its absence. Along with chests of drawers, bedside cabinets and a large wall-mounted television situated in the master bedroom, there was also an electric log effect fire situated underneath it.

An unusual feature in a bedroom, but it adds character to the large airy room. There was a bath with a shower over, a washbasin and a toilet. The washbasin had under storage shelving and a large mirror sat on the wall directly above it. All standard and all good. Access to the bathroom was via two entrances. Firstly from the good-sized hallway on the second floor, and secondly from the connecting doors located in the master bedroom.

There were locks on both doors, ensuring neither Jackie nor Claire could accidentally walk in whilst they were sitting on the toilet doing their business! What a sight for sore eyes that would be, despite being sisters.

A largish storage cupboard in the hallway, when opened, revealed clean surplus towels, hand and bath variations, and flannels galore. Spare bedding in abundance and extra duvets and pillows; just in case they had had extra visitors, they presumed. All appeared to be thought out thoroughly and the girls couldn't have been more delighted. Well done, Mark and Louise; a thumbs-up to them both.

Jackie, being curious, had vetted the back garden, located through a side gate. She just had to investigate, her nature for sure. There appeared to be an apartment at the basement level and she felt that she shouldn't have been "snooping", so to speak. From the outside looking in, it definitely looked lived in. The wellington boots and trainers on the porchway more or less confirmed it.

There was a garage next to the grassy area, a small lawned piece of ground; it looked unused, there for storage and not much else. Parking a car in it, the general use for a garage hadn't always warranted it being used for that purpose. In this instance, that had been the case. Jackie hadn't felt comfortable and quickly returned to the house, closing the side gate behind her.

Advising Claire that the back of the house appeared to be off-limits, no clothesline to use either, her cigarettes had required smoking on the steps, the access to the front door, instead. There wasn't a back door, so it was what it was. Whether she could have partaken the habit inside, Jackie hadn't known, but her sister had always smoked outside in hers and John's own home; nothing needed changing on that score.

As the sisters started unpacking, a knock on the door stopped play, so to speak. Claire's unpacking was done and she was attempting to make a cup of tea for them both in the kitchen area of the downstairs open-plan room. Without a suitcase to open, the holdall had taken mere minutes to reassemble in the master bedroom. Jackie chose the smaller of the three bedrooms and was in the throes of hanging up some of her garments in one of Claire's wardrobes when she answered the door.

Mark walked through the door holding a box of "goodies" for them. Everything from fresh milk, sugar and teabags, to breakfast cereal, bacon and eggs. Cheese, sliced ham, bread, butter, yoghurts, and chocolate. The girls had told him off initially but were so glad of the food. Jackie had brought teabags, sweeteners and powdered milk with her from the UK. Claire's attempt at a decent cuppa beforehand had now appeared in the form of Mark (their guardian angel), and they were oh so grateful.

A cup of English breakfast tea was a life-saver, one they couldn't do without.

The hugs began between him and the girls; he was so pleased to see them both. He was soon to be married to the love of his life, but his family was important to him and it showed. He was elated to see them, as the girls were to indeed see him. Conversation had resulted in Claire disclosing that her suitcase had disappeared; somewhere between Gatwick airport and Calgary airport, she'd informed him.

She'd lost her wedding outfit, amongst other things. Wedding presents from herself and other family members unable to be there for the celebration were also lost in the luggage carrier.

Mark was instantly on the phone to Louise; help was required, of the female kind. Clothes for Claire until the suitcase had shown up being prioritised. He quickly ran through the vicinities in walking distance from the house and there was a row of small shops very nearby; something the sisters had required checking on. Only general stores, Mark had said; large retail outlets were car rides away, rather than walking distance.

Louise was calling in the following morning and escorting them to a large department store, one on the lines of Debenhams and John Lewis in the UK. An outlet that sold almost everything, including the kitchen sink! Claire's response was euphoric, so excited. Louise was a life-saver, for sure. The suitcase was still missing, but first things first, Jackie's sibling loved clothes shopping.

It was no hardship, not really. A shopping spree whilst in Canada, why not? Mark had given out more hugs as he headed for his home, and promised to be in touch soon. He also added that there was an apartment at the back of the house that was occupied. The rear of the property was out of bounds for them. Jackie hadn't told him that she'd already investigated the area. They both knew the score now and the house was more than adequate for them; it could have occupied a few more relatives, in fact.

Settling down after their long journey, a hot bath was something they both relished. Total relaxation in preparation for the week ahead. What was in store for them, they both questioned? Nothing was ever plain sailing; that was way too easy. Taking it in turn, the hot water was filling the bath up, ready for a few moments of spa experience; though without the bubbles. They could pretend, couldn't they?

Jackie changed into her nightwear, and thankfully, she'd packed two pairs of pyjamas. Claire was dressed in her spare pair after her leisurely bath.

'Where's the hair-dryer?' Claire shouted down to her sister from the bathroom.

'I've not seen one,' Jackie replied. She hadn't looked for one either, not given it a thought.

Hunt the hair-dryer resulted in one not being found. Neither of them had packed one, as the Deer Lodge was equipped with one in each room of the building. Claire, if she had done so, wouldn't have helped the situation; not with the clothes carrier disappearing into thin air. A hair-dryer added itself to the list of purchases the next day. Girls couldn't manage without something that could dry their wet hair, no way. Sisters! Could anything else go wrong?

Both Mark and Louise were career people and had studied hard to get where they are today. Louise was still in the throes of studying to become a General Practitioner in Canada. Now in her late twenties, she was almost there. Mark, on the other hand, had served in the British Armed Forces and experienced Afghanistan at its worst. Not a good experience.

After finishing in the forces, he enrolled in an environmental degree at Swansea university in South Wales. Louise had been studying there too, after successfully being accepted as an exchange student. They met, fell in love and the rest is history, as they say.

Mark decided to make his home in Canada, Louise's residence and birthplace. Who wouldn't? Given the choices available. He secured a job there and they bought their first property, a house in Edmonton. The road had been a long one, as far as university and studying were concerned, but they were now where they both wanted to be and couldn't be happier or more contented. Marriage was the next step on the ladder, sealing their love and commitment to one another.

A story book romance that probably shouldn't have evolved, but did. Across the miles, their love blossomed when Louise was forced to return home on occasion, due to protocol (her visa had required renewing). Theirs was a true fairytale ending, with a full life ahead of them, still. All good there, and to the girls, a true love story.

Mark missed his family back in the UK, that was obvious. Having some of his family there to witness the marriage was preferential to none of them, and both Mark and Louise fully understood the absences, for one reason or another. Life could get in the way of things, and occasions had often gone ahead without some people specifically wanting there. Life wasn't an open book, sadly.

Both had known that they would see their UK family members at some point, later rather than sooner; here and there, near and far, living at its best for sure. Christmas was six months away yet, plenty of time for them to make the journey across the miles themselves, as a newly married couple.

Finances aside, meetings would occur between the family members eventually, those concerned. The girls had eaten well that evening, choosing some of the food that Mark had so kindly delivered to them. Deciphering the workings of the television and its remote and finding a suitable programme to watch was Claire's domain. Jackie would have given up far too quickly, resorting to reading or glancing at her phone instead; there was always the game of Candy Crush.

Claire managed to find a movie channel, which they watched until bedtime had arrived. Louise was picking them up early the next morning for a shopping extravaganza and they were both looking forward to it; excited in fact. Had they never shopped before? Well, not in that part of Canada.

Jackie always ensured that her walking stick was at hand, folded neatly into her handbag. Her walking mobility could change dramatically, forcing her to use it or rest for a while. Either way, she was always prepared. Not bringing a large enough handbag with her, Jackie noted two purchases in her head, a larger handbag and a hair-dryer. Could she remember them in the morning, though?

Edmonton took the forefront now, after the previous days at Lake Louise, and it was only day one of a whole week's exploring. There was so much more to come, they both knew. For Jackie, the experiences so far would hold precious memories, along with disappointment at not having Alan there with her. He would have congratulated her on being there without him, knowing full well that if the roles were reversed, and she'd sadly passed on prior to him, he'd not have entered into the vacation.

Brave, Jackie wasn't. Realistic though, she was. Alan would have wanted her to continue the holidays they had both thoroughly revelled in, some spent with Claire and John over the years. Mobility aside, Claire's sister hadn't wanted to remain stagnant in the house, twiddling her thumbs until her days were over. She could relax when she'd died, peacefully.

Banff, Jasper and Sun Peaks were recollections of the past, all good ones. A fortieth wedding anniversary vacation that exceeded all expectations had come to mind. Not being big earners on the career front, Jackie and Alan's earnings were mediocre compared to the majority of others around. In all honesty, they'd probably had less than two brain cells between them; never the brightest of the bunch.

Somehow, Jackie managed to save for a holiday of a lifetime; forty years of marriage was worth celebrating, in her eyes anyway. Today, she realised that they were never going to celebrate their fiftieth, well not together. They would have splashed out on a landmark occasion for definite. Finances aside, it was never going to happen. Miracles did occur but not of this kind.

The Canadian experience, the Rockies, was only part of the adventure then. The tip of the iceberg, the highlight of the holiday, was a week's luxury cruise in Alaska. Cold as it was, the glaciers passed by as all on board clicked away at the sights seen from the cruise ship. A sight for sore eyes, no, an awe-inspiring experience not to be missed; along with Jackie's hopes of actually reaching their fortieth wedding anniversary. It hadn't been guaranteed.

They had, with uncertainty, achieved that goal and the expectations were well beyond anticipation. Alaska was beautiful, the people were friendly and helpful, and Jackie's dream had come true, against all the odds. Memories of the vacation were as alert as ever, no clouds covering the out of this world trip abroad.

Little was she to know that things were to change in the future, dramatically; not for the better, unfortunately. Shortly after their Canadian/Alaskan adventure, Alan's health had shown signs of concern. Not related to the vacation at all, but sadly, a terminal diagnosis that wasn't going to go away. It hadn't, but Jackie's recollections of their precious moments at the time were still there. So clear, it was as if it had occurred just yesterday.

Expensive as it was, she'd been so glad that they had celebrated their marriage on something as luxurious as the holiday itself. Just riding the huskies through the forest was worth doing, and getting to know the well-behaved dogs personally. One of the dogs, a black husky, was called Thomas, Jackie and Alan's son's name. She had laughed to herself momentarily.

The extra paid to have a balcony suite with a jacuzzi bath as standard was immaterial now. Sometimes, just sometimes, it was worth throwing caution to the wind. Memories were there for life, and Jackie's mind had gone back to that time, with smiles adorning her face; before falling asleep that evening.

Chapter Twelve

They were both up early and raring to go. Well, that was a bit of an exaggeration but the sisters were looking forward to shopping and seeing more of Canada; anything else was a bonus.

Delighting in the experience was a priority, a new one to them both. Excitement overload at a large department store, something that Jackie had usually abstained from, stayed away from back home. There was no fun in it when on your own.

Louise picked them up early, as promised. The journey hadn't taken that long and driving to the large department store, to her, was easy enough; Jackie tried to memorise the journey but with roundabouts and lanes in multitude, she'd never have mastered it. Living in the location was obviously an advantage, but with driving on the right-hand side of the road and roundabouts being complicated as a result, an accident waiting to happen had sprung to mind.

Leave it to the experts had Jackie's mind registering. Taxis and family transport would be the next week's way of travelling, for sure.

Very similar to John Lewis and Debenhams back home, the department store was equipped with several floors of goods, all separated into specific compartments selling similar products. Shoes and bags, clothing of all variations; sportswear, designer gear, and general everyday ranges. Perfumes and make-up, in abundance; all too numerous to name individually, some brands never heard of before.

Home-ware of all descriptions, all expertly laid out for customers to browse at their own pace, tempting them to purchase and part with their monies. The store was huge and never-ending, it seemed.

There were several sets of escalators there to take you up and down the floors with ease; the only other option being numerous flights of stairs. Claire loved the store, deciding where to look first, with Louise's help. Clothing items were urgently needed, including underwear, a must. A handbag and make-up, and toiletries. All were safely stored in her suitcase, somewhere around about!

Jackie didn't require any more clothes but that didn't stop her from buying another top to add to her collection. A larger bag was found, but not easily; the majority around were well overpriced and although Claire's sister could afford to pay the price tag, morally she'd refused to allow herself to part with the monies asked. A rip-off came to mind.

The much-needed hair-dryer was found after asking the assistant for a less expensive replica of the one on display. How much? Jackie had shrieked on seeing the price of the one positioned centre stage. With electrical connections being different in Canada and the UK, the dryer for hair would be a useless purchase if taken back home with them. So why pay above the odds?

Claire's wardrobe was slowly being added to, necessities and a dress for the wedding celebration. There still had been no luck with her suitcase's whereabouts, sadly, and the dress was a "just in case" item. Mark was on the case, so to speak. He was probably in contact with the airport as they were indeed shopping. Another voice couldn't do any harm, could it?

The store had several eateries in evidence. The majority of famous take-away outlets known worldwide were there. Who hadn't heard of McDonald's, Subway and Burger King; Krispy Kreme Donuts and Kentucky Fried Chicken to name two more? There were other eateries there, Canada's equivalent of ones in the UK, but Louise and the girls settled for a Subway roll, and Mark's fiancée had treated them to a cinnamon donut each.

A very moreish sweet desert and deliciously tasty, finger-licking good. Take-away coffees had complimented their lunch, Costa Coffee no less. Once satisfied with their purchases, they all headed towards Louise's car, homeward bound. Thanking them for their company, Louise headed back to her own house, promising to see them both soon. The girls hadn't realised just how soon.

A day out they both had, and anything else occurring that day would have been unexpected. They were both content with their day, for sure.

Claire tried on her new clothing again once back in the house. She nodded with approval. Jackie, on the other hand, had been confident enough by just looking at her new top; she was certain it would fit fine. Once put on for an evening out, she would know for certain. It hadn't cost a fortune, so Jackie had hedged her bets. Was she being a tad lazy? Probably, she thought to herself.

A cup of tea was desperately due, so Jackie filled the kettle with water and put it on to boil. Two cups were prepared and carried over to the coffee table as they both sat down on the large sofa. Resting their legs and bodies, the hot liquid was nectar to the Gods as they drank their cuppas. With minds wondering what to prepare for their evening meal, or to dial in a take-away supper, Claire's phone had rang.

It was Mark, informing her that he'd contacted Calgary airport about her suitcase, giving a full description of the luggage carrier to the person on the other end of the phone. Nothing had been found fitting the description but they would keep looking. He'd also said that he would be picking them up in a few hours' time, taking them to his home for a barbecue evening.

Louise's family would be there to meet them, joining in the evening, they'd both been informed. Jackie hadn't met her relatives beforehand, so this was all new to her. Louise's parents had visited the UK before, meeting up with Claire and John, and Claire's children and grandchildren; they weren't complete strangers. Jackie was a little nervous if she was honest.

There was another member of the family Mark desperately wanted them to meet. Their pet pooch, Alfie, was their world. A pup still, a large one at that, similar to a young child; very busy and full of pent-up energy. He was their baby and spoilt rotten. Par for the course where animals and children were concerned. Who couldn't love them?

It was time for a bath, to wash their hair and try out the new hair-dryer, before deciding what to put on for the outdoor occasion. The weather was hot and sunny and should remain so until late evening. Warm clothing wasn't necessary, but maybe a cardigan, just in case. Better to be safe than sorry! Jackie had pondered awhile before deciding one way or another.

Amelia's words rang in Jackie's ear. The girls' mother was always a chilly person and where others wore sleeveless clothing in the sunshine, she would be seen with a thick knitted cardigan over her summer dress. Thinking about her mum when packing her suitcase, Jackie ensured that a few long-sleeved items, of sorts, were included. A mother's instinct, maybe. Was it thinking about Alan as well that made Jackie pack for all weathers, in June?

A creature of habit, he was also a cold person, and did not have a lot of fat on his lean body. Not for lack of eating, Alan could eat for England and Wales; though probably not for Canada, their portions being way too big. He would have given it a go, regardless. John, on the other hand, would have succeeded where Alan would have failed. John's build and height were complete opposites, and probably why.

Whatever made Jackie pack knitted garments, or whoever, Jackie had been grateful for. A barbecue evening could last well into the night and become colder as the time elapsed. A cover-up was essential, and luckily, she'd packed a spare; one for Claire to wear if needed later on during their evening outside.

Mark had picked them up on cue and they were both ready for an evening with family members, along with food and drink included. Socialising at its best, they both agreed. He was keen to show them his and Louise's home, and more importantly, the baby of the family, Alfie, the dog. The pup sounded adorable and mischievous, as all younger dogs were.

The excitement was obvious in Mark, and his nerves calmed down after everything wedding related had been fully completed. All the boxes had been ticked and the "I's" all dotted. He could now relax a little, and today was about just that, relaxing with family. It had been a lot to do and mentally exhausting, but everything had to be right for the big day. No calamities were allowed. There were others attending the wedding celebration who also lived in the UK.

Family members that Jackie hadn't known. They were familiar to Claire though, but had arranged their holiday itinerary and accommodation separately from theirs. Some were more familiar than others to Claire, so the get-together would be a lot easier. Not being complete strangers would definitely help the evening where the conversation was concerned.

Jackie, on first encounters, wasn't the most talkative person around; further meetings along though, she would usually ease up and talk for England. Ask any of her family and friends! There was no stopping her once she'd gotten to know someone but the first impressions of her character insinuated a quiet and reserved individual. Definitely a misdiagnosis there.

The car journey hadn't taken more than ten minutes. Their home was within walking distance from where Claire and Jackie were staying, but Jackie and directions wouldn't have led her there by her own steam. Her sister would have found it, she was certain, but whether they would have found their way back to where they were staying, was debatable. If left to Jackie's recollections, then no would have been the answer. Allowing Mark to pick them both up was the right thing to do, the best decision. Safety first in a strange country.

Streets and cul-de-sacs were passed by. Jackie noted that the houses had all appeared to be of the detached type. No terraced or semi-detached properties, all in abundance in the UK. Each and every house in Edmonton had space around them, some more than others. Front and back gardens, some had one or the other, and a few had both. The house the girls were in had only a back garden, with a tree-lined avenue and fair-sized pavements to the front of the property.

Mark and Louise lived in a cul-de-sac and their house had garage space to the front of the property. He parked in the garage and the three of them walked into the house via the garage entrance. They were the first there, so Mark gave them a tour of the house. It was large in comparison to most back home, but not huge. A desirable property with more than enough space and adequate rooms for a family later on in their marriage.

Having its own office room was a definite advantage in today's times. With a huge majority of jobs becoming home-based and requiring to be office equipped, the room was becoming mandatory in the world as it is now. A lot of the UK's properties were older residences and didn't have the space to accommodate a room to be used solely as an office. Many of the newer built constructions included a study as a matter of course.

The garden was at the back, through the kitchen area, and was of a good size. Mainly laid to grass, there was a raised decking area seating a good many people. Mark and Louise placed buckets filled with cans and bottles of drink, soft and alcoholic variations on the decking area. The barbecue was already positioned in preparation for the cooking of barbecued goodies, burgers and sausages mainly.

A fold-up table was opened and set up, filled with homemade salads of various mixtures, bread rolls, sauces and other appetisers, all to everyone's tastes. The girls were impressed and said so to Mark. Louise was collecting Alfie from the sitter and emerged with the pup in tow as they settled on seats outside. He, like all animals, wanted to be made a fuss of; the girls obliged willingly.

Of the larger breed of dog, and still not fully grown, Alfie wasn't an animal that could hide in some inconspicuous corner unseen. Not of the toy breed, but larger than life, and equally adorable and infectious. Jackie had loved dogs, but after losing her beloved "Sally", a Heinz variety, when in her twenties, she'd never wanted to own a dog of her own. Sally was the family pet and is still missed today; there whilst the siblings had grown up, from very small children.

The family home wasn't the same without Sally (as well as Freddie, the tortoise and Fluffy and Tiny, the resident cats). The thought of losing a dog of her own was similar to losing a loved one.

By default, she'd inherited a kitten. She was there, on the main road, and hadn't belonged to anyone. Jackie's daughter had brought it into the house and it remained there for twenty years. A fluffy ball of a cat, loved as a child would have been treated, equally the same. After contracting cancer in her face and passing away two decades later, Jackie poured her heart out. Since then, living on her own was preferential to going through anything similar again.

Alfie was gorgeous, nevertheless, and pampering him the girls both did until more bodies entered the house; they'd taken over then and the barbecue was in full swing at last. Conversation and eating took precedence with Alfie there joining in, he wasn't excluded from the celebration; a joining of family members from home and afar.

Chapter Thirteen

From just Mark, Louise and them, Jackie and Claire, the garden was suddenly filled with bodies. People Jackie had never met; it was nerve-racking and daunting at first. Louise's parents were lovely people, her father being a quiet soul with minimum conversation. He preferred being in the background and out of sight. Jackie's make-up had been similar, not wanting to stand out amongst the crowd, ever.

Her mother, on the other hand, was the exact opposite. She revelled in mixing with everyone there, so loving the physical presence. She could have spoken for Canada, all in a nice way. Being so excited about meeting the visitors from the UK, she wanted to know everything about her soon-to-be family members from afar. All completely normal and everyone willingly answered any questions asked and gave more.

Louise's sister and husband were both friendly and made them feel welcome there. Expecting her first baby in a few months' time, Alexandra was still working full-time in the hospital and was getting tired easily. Steven, her husband, looked the typical Canadian; if Canada had indeed had a type that was.

Andrew, their older brother, and his wife were busy with their girls. They had two young daughters, and did say hello, introducing themselves as part of the family. Louise's brother was your typical bodybuilder with thick dark hair and a beard; tall and solid, with the Canadian accent heard around the area. A gentle giant came to mind.

Jackie had no clue as to what he did for a living, but if guessed would have gone down the route of a forestry technician or a rig manager. She could envisage him felling down trees in the forest with a chain saw in hand and dressed in rugged clothing and a red checked shirt. Equally, Claire's sister could see Andrew clearly working on an oil rig, his hands covered in the thick black liquid and pulling at the heavy chains.

Probably completely way off the scale, Jackie couldn't imagine him working inside or in the computer industry. His build and look shouted out an outdoor career. She could have been completely wrong, and usually was, but if looks had defined a career, then that's where he would have belonged. What did Jackie know?

Mark's mother, stepfather, and his daughter from a previous relationship, were settled at the far end of the decking area. Claire was familiar with them but that was about it. With them was Mark's brother and his wife, Chris and Molly. The girls had known the latter well. The group of people had all travelled together from the UK and were sharing accommodation in Edmonton.

Mark was busy cooking the food on the barbecue as everyone helped themselves to drink from the buckets around. Conversation continued for hours and hours, from one person to another and back again. The food was devoured quickly and Mark continued to cook until everybody was satisfied, full to the brim and unable to move. Mark and Louise's hard work had paid off.

As the sky turned black and the temperature became colder, those remaining at the end of the evening ventured inside the house. The lounge area was now full of bums on seats and conversation continued until the early hours of the morning. Tiredness hadn't happened, there was so much to talk about; the wedding being a major talking point.

When Mark finally returned them to the house they were staying in, they thanked him for a lovely time. They had meant every word of it. He smiled and waved before heading back to his home, presumably to clear up! Jackie, for one, couldn't have rested and gone to bed until all was back to normal. Mark's stance on that, she'd not been sure of.

Venturing to the shops the next day, the local shops in walking distance, was a must on both of the sisters' list of to-dos. Exploring the area itself just had to be done. The chances of them ever revisiting Edmonton, or indeed Canada, weren't promised. A residential area it was, but your general "corner" shop had to be seen and purchases made and paid for. It was compulsory!

Checking as to whether their prices were higher than the supermarkets of Canada wasn't something they would know about, not having experienced the large food shops around about. Comparing goods to British prices was a talking point though, for future reference. Was the cost of living better there than back home?

When Alan and Jackie holidayed in Toronto, years back, they were surprised at the lower than expected cost of goods there. Food eateries, clothing and footwear, as well as jewellery; Alan had bought his wife an eternity ring there, at the end of the holiday. There had been monies remaining on the final day, not a usual occurrence.

The sun was still shining as they strolled from the house to the retail area, just a five minute walk away. All the streets appeared identical, houses being all pretty much the same. A few had children's toys parked outside their front doors; small bicycles with stabilisers, dolls prams and the like. Toys of the metal and plastic variations that would stand the time of different weathers: sunshine, snow and rain. Proof that there were children residing in houses in the neighbourhood.

Not seeing any children around whilst walking, it was nice to know that they existed. It was a school day, so many would have been there being educated, and babies sleeping inside their homes, presumably. A seemingly quiet neighbourhood, the streets were clean and debris-free.

Always a good sign of a good location.

Jackie's bugbear had always been the graffiti scribbled on house and garden walls, as well as street pavements. Artistic perhaps, but in her eyes, it lowered the tone of the district. Her opinion, but nevertheless; surely creations of these sorts should be painted or sketched on paper or canvas. Maybe Jackie was a snob!

Tattoos on people's bodies, her stance on them was a negative one. Babies weren't born with tattoos, so why plaster your body with ink? At a push, one was okay, but Jackie drew the line at covering large areas of the person with ink impressions. The pain endured would have put her off, any roads. Creativity at its best, graffiti and tattoos held no space in her life.

There were no sightings of anything graffiti-based, all good. A few seats were dotted around the entrance to the shopping part of the district, now in evidence in front of their eyes. Claire and Jackie both headed for the general store, the mini-market, the corner shop; several names denoting the retail establishment there. The convenience store was another name for the type of outlet it was.

Claire had espied the sweet and chocolate range, as well as purchasing cigarettes ensuring she hadn't run out whilst in Edmonton. Jackie walked around every aisle of the store, slowly browsing the products on offer. She picked up some fancy cakes to delight in with a cup of tea when back at the house. Picking up a lottery ticket and hoping her luck was in, Jackie had hedged her bets.

Luck wasn't something that came naturally to her, but had decided to have a go anyway.

Taking in the variation of retail outlets in the rank, there was a hairdresser, a small cafe, a pharmacist and two takeaways opposite the general store, directly across the road. A little further down was a bakery shop, an acupuncture and back pain specialist; a chiropractic, she thought it was called. Another similar building was next to it, obviously of the health and beauty type.

An alcohol shop there was of a good size. Selling everything relating to the consumption of beers, lagers and spirits, they appeared to have a good trade. Yet another take-away establishment was adjacent to the "booze" shop, and where later on in the week, the girls would tempt their palate and try a meal there.

There was also another hairdresser tucked in behind the rank of shops, and Jackie so needed a haircut. An appointment would be made there soon, she told herself. Claire wasn't averse to having her fingernails and toenails prettied up either. Jackie's nails were never polished, well her toenails were occasionally; usually when venturing abroad for a short vacation. Alan had always hated nail polished fingernails, screwing up his nose on seeing them on the ladies, and even more so the men.

An expensive hobby today, Jackie abstained and did not venture down that road. She hated being pampered, her worst nightmare if she was totally honest. Having her hair cut was done as and when required only. It hadn't been an occasion she had ever been enthusiastic about. Needs must and all that, the less fuss the better where Claire's sister was concerned.

A steady walk back to the house was done, recognising the houses with the children's toys outside. A pointer as to the correct route to the street where they were residing. Jackie and directions were never the best, absolutely deplorable if she was completely honest. Recalling driving to destinations without too much difficulty, actually returning afterwards and memorising the way back, had never panned out. Where she ended up beforehand wasn't something planned but a mystery tour in the making, for sure.

As the week progressed, she decided on a walk alone; spending a few hours in her own company. Claire was more than happy to remain in the house, pampering herself in a luxurious bath and listening to music or watching the television (if she could work out the channels that was).

She'd not been concerned about Jackie going out alone, and had no reason to.

Jackie found the shops, enjoyed a large latte in the small cafe and was given directions to two local parks in the vicinity. Content to walk slowly down the road given, both parks were found without too much trouble. Jackie spent a while admiring the recreational parks and watching the children release their energy in happy play. There was a small lake opposite one of them, a relaxing experience; photos were a must for memory's sake.

She continued walking, passing house after house after house. A large retail park was seen across a main busy road. Everything needed for people living in the locality; from eateries to clothes shops, to home essentials. Probably a lot more besides but Jackie hadn't ventured across the road to see more. She found a seat and rested awhile, deliberating as to whether to proceed any further on her journey. Discovering Edmonton on foot was good for exercising and much more.

Deciding to return to the house, she turned around, walking back the same route that she had come, or so she'd thought. Where Jackie went wrong, she did not know. The parks and small lake had disappeared completely. They were nowhere to be seen. A mystery, for certain. For a time, Jackie was totally flummoxed and in the dark. Claire's sister was lost and not for the first time.

Looking at her watch, the time was flying by and Mark was picking them both up for a second barbecue evening; this time at Louise's parents' home. Jackie needed to get back but couldn't recall the name of the street they were staying at. 'A brain full of sawdust,' she'd uttered to herself. Writing it down somewhere would have been very practical, just in case!

Continuing the walk, a gentleman on a bicycle rode by and Jackie called out to him for help. There was nothing wrong with her voice, just her directions. Asking the whereabouts of the small cafe (she'd managed to remember its name), the gentleman in question told her that she had walked two blocks further than required.

Canada's streets were arranged in blocks, as were residential areas in the USA. Having holidayed in the USA in the past, Jackie was familiar with blocked areas and turned around, marching along the road at speed before turning after the two blocks had passed. Suddenly, the parks were seen, the lake and finally, the cafe. Phew!

Jackie arrived back to the house with half an hour to spare before Mark had picked them up in his car. Disappointed with herself, she did not divulge the reason for being so long to her sister. Had she panicked? Of course, she had. Getting lost in Canada was an experience not to be repeated, and she hadn't, thankfully.

Chapter Fourteen

Louise's parents' home was beautiful; large in comparison to most residences, but warm and welcoming. Most of the UK visitors were there to experience the barbecue, along with their own family members. Pretty much the same bodies as at Mark and Louise's house with exactly the same ambience as before.

There was no expense spared where food was concerned. Prepared salad variations, steak succulently cooked on the barbecue along with other meats and variations of barbecued foods: pork, chicken, burgers and sausages. The amount of prepared eateries was endless and never-ending, and all absolutely delicious. Cake variations after the main meal were displayed in the kitchen area at the large house. All looking mouth-wateringly good and moreish. So difficult to choose just one dessert.

Alcohol was in abundance. If Louise's mother had been allowed to, every single person there (except the children that was) would have been totally inebriated, for sure. The bar of different alcoholic drinks there was brimming with spirits and beer, most of them Jackie had never heard of. Frankie (her real name was Frances) wanted everyone there to try each and every one of the bottles on the shelf and had failed miserably in succeeding.

The evening had gone on forever, it seemed. Bodies were moving from the garden to inside the house and back again. Donald, Don for short, concerned himself over the girls' bare feet in the garden. Armed with two pairs of his socks, he issued each of them with a pair to wear for fear of their feet getting cold. Such a thoughtful person, Louise's dad was definitely someone to admire and liken to. A caring nature always, the girls had adorned the socks throughout the evening. Their feet were toasty, no argument there!

Everything in the house shouted out wealth. There probably were items purchased in the dollar shop, but nothing in view had stood out. Both of Louise's parents had held down good jobs in the past, Don still working but due to retire soon. The welcome from the family though, was anything but posh. Down to earth since meeting them earlier, nothing indicated anything different in their own home.

Conversation was in abundance, with music in the background creating a lovely atmosphere. The fear of dropping something valuable or touching ornaments within easy reach wasn't there; pins couldn't be heard dropping amongst the crowd there. Both Jackie and Claire felt comfortable the entire evening, with smiles on their faces throughout. Louise was a lucky lady, having such devoted and laid-back parents.

Both Jackie's and Claire's homes would have fitted into the first floor and basement of Frankie and Don's house, and there was still a third floor that neither of them had ventured upon. Property aside, they could have been living in a converted stable (Frankie had bred horses in her youth) and the atmosphere wouldn't have been any different. Proof that everything wasn't always about money.

Photographs of the three children growing up, their two granddaughters and family images, adorned the living area of the house. Proud parents showing off their offspring. Jackie's living room incorporated the same. Her two children and five grandsons were her pride and joy and always would be. They needed to be there on display.

Memories depicting their growth over the years were something valued and so worth portraying. Rich or poor, living the same values in completely different residences. Life meant nothing different to the majority of living beings. Family is and always will be the most important word in the dictionary. Without them, the world would be in a sorry state of affairs. Jackie would have been lost, without a doubt.

Mark made a trip to Calgary airport in the hope that Claire's suitcase had been found and had suddenly reappeared. The men in the family required slight adjustments to their wedding suits, so the journey itself hadn't been going out of his way. The result wasn't positive, it hadn't miraculously been discovered. Mark gave his mobile phone number as an extra link in the hope of the clothes carrier coming to light.

Had Claire given up on getting her belongings back? She'd not said anything to Jackie, one way or another. The conversation hadn't arisen, and neither of them instigated one. It was a sore subject if Jackie was honest. Claire hadn't required a reminder, that was for sure. Possessions were just materialistic but losing them wasn't something anyone would have wished for.

The following days passed by quickly. Jackie managed to have her hair cut and Claire's fingernails and toenails were reinvented with a different colour. Her bright orange nails no longer matched the wedding attire she was going to wear on the big day. Her newly purchased outfits required newly polished nails of a different colour scheme. This time, it was white and Claire was pleased with the results.

There were more meet-ups with the family, for meals out in eateries nearby, more conversation and getting to know the relatives more intimately. It was a roller-coaster of hugs every time they met up. All good in the context of things. People become familiar with those across the miles, those that would remain in their hearts and minds yet seldom see face to face in the future.

Making the most of the occasion was what it was all about and nobody was complaining. A trip to Fort Edmonton, a park filled with history going back to the early 1900s, was something done by the sisters. A taxi there and back, the experience was well worth the monies paid at the gate. The old fairground of years gone by, nothing that dangerous in today's terms but entertaining nevertheless.

Knocking the coconut off its stand with a lightweight plastic ball had appeared easy enough, but when actioned was a lot harder than it had looked. Hooking a duck with a prize attached; accomplishing it wasn't "easy peasy" either. The turntable was continuously moving, so grabbing a hold onto any hook was a miracle in itself, nearly impossible.

Alan had loved the grabbers in the amusement arcades, concentrating on cornering a soft toy for his children when younger, and now his grandsons. These days, the chance of actually picking one up and depositing it into the hold was virtually off-limits. Either the toys were too bulky and too heavy or the grabber itself wouldn't close enough to contain the soft toy for more than a few seconds.

Money was lost in the attempts to win something, but the excitement held a concentrated enthusiasm at the time. The whole idea of the game, encouraging people to part with their hard-earned cash and spending some happy memories in the process, wasn't altogether bad news. Life wasn't always meant to be dull and boring.

The streets of earlier days held incredible memories of life gone by. The old chapel stood resplendent, with aged rugs on the bare wooden floors. The alter was there, pride of place, to recite the words of the Bible to its congregation; attending on a Sunday was almost mandatory back then. Families met up most Sundays after chapel for a few moments of conversation, asking about each other's families, their health and well-being.

The bakery shop was wafting out the smell of freshly cooked bread, lovingly packaged and sold to visitors as it would have in its heyday. It certainly made the girls feel hungry. The old oven still worked, proving that newer creations were there for the woman of today, but the lady of the house in the earlier years could still produce edible foods for the larger families of the era.

A longer process, maybe, the old-fashioned and rather antiquated and bulky-looking contraptions had done their jobs admirably. Wow…that bread smelled so tempting. Jackie imagined dipping it into a hearty bowl of beef stew and dumplings. She suddenly realised just how hungry she actually was and walked into the bakery to purchase one of the loaves of bread on display.

The old vehicles of the day were there on display, immaculately presented and shining with a recognition of importance. The motorbike and sidecar, even older than the one Jackie recalled her own dad owning, represented a part of history that time had passed by. There was something about looking at the transport in the early 1900s; big, bold and yet beautiful. The workmanship was immaculate.

Jackie remembered the numerous Morris Minors and Morris 1000s that Alan had driven over the years. A company car if you like, part of his salary in the foundry he had worked in since leaving school at fifteen until its closure some twenty-five years later. Luxury cars they weren't but a convenient run of the mill make of vehicle at the time. He had a few Morris Travellers as well, now a popular vintage and sought-after model worth a lot of money in today's terms.

'How things were taken for granted,' she said out loud. 'It was merely a way of getting around and nothing more.'

If the vehicles on display could have spoken, they would have revelled in the fashion parade, proud to be ogled by so many people. Vanity at its best and well worthy of being there. Historical presents to treasure, so to speak and spectacular in their own right. Who would argue the case? The photographs taken were proof in themselves.

The tram had taken people from one street in time to another year; the changes noticed being mindful of the less privileged and their way of living. A tent complete with bedroom furniture and a metal bucket and bowl used to bathe one's body. A cold feeling had taken over the sisters' arms and legs; the thought itself sent shivers down their spines. How lucky were they today?

The uprising costs of heating a home along with the family bathroom caused financial problems of late but at least their bathroom or washing area, was inside four walls rather than a flimsy cloth tent. Winter must have been unbearable; just thinking about it was frightening. They must have been frozen to the bone. Jackie's teeth had chattered with the cold there and then, her mind back there in times gone by.

As Jackie put on her fourth layer of clothing to cut the energy bills down, a recap of the women of the 1900s attire had been recalled. No wonder they had dressed from head to toe in long dresses made from warm winter materials, with thick woollen stockings underneath and a head covered in a bonnet for warmth. They needed it. There was never much skin showing outside their clothing; their face, hands and shoe-covered feet as a rule. Dressed for the weather, they were the sensible ones. No doubt about it.

The teenagers of today looked frozen to the core in minuscule skirts and dresses, with their bare arms and legs showing to all the world in winter! Crazy was just one word that came to mind. What would grandmother have said? Even back when Jackie was a teenager, Thomas, her dad, would have ordered her to go back upstairs and put some clothes on! Not because she would have frozen outside of the house but because of the way she had looked. The Red Light District came to mind!

The tram took them to yet another year, later than the last one and people in period costumes had walked the street as they would have way back then. Ladies carrying their wicker baskets laden with home-baked (well, shop-baked on the premises) goods along with fresh fruit and vegetables. Items necessary to prepare an evening meal for the family. Supermarket shopping had never existed then.

Life was busy but each family member had their jobs to do, a routine done without any sign of disobedience. Children would never argue with their elders, ever. How different things are today?

There were a few buildings selling vintage memorabilia, items obsolete now but essential in years gone by. Claire had browsed the items on display and purchased a few things; Jackie concentrated on reading the plaque outside, information about the history of the building in question. It used to be a school there for the younger children of the era. Interesting, very interesting.

Claire's sister savoured being educated about the way people had lived in the past and wondered how she herself would have coped, way back then. With Jackie's luck, back in the day, she would have been one of the servants and Claire would have secured the position of lady of the house. Even as children, Claire's luck was always superior to her older sister's. Jackie's life wouldn't have appeared any easier than that of today.

As the sisters walked out of the gates and headed for a taxi to take them back to the house, they both agreed that the day had positive vibes and was a truly magical and educational experience, a history lesson on Canada's past. Awesome, in fact. There had been so much to take in and digest; the sisters were forever learning.

Chapter Fifteen

The week in Edmonton had flown by, it seemed. Packed and ready for the next and final part of the journey, an area known as Canmore, the girls were picked up by Louise's mum, Frances (or Frankie as she was known). They were to travel with her to their next destination, a three to four hour trip.

Chester passed Canmore several times, on the dual carriageway that was, but they'd not gone through the area at all; literally bypassed it on their journeys through Canada. A pit stop for lunch, after Frankie had stopped at the shopping mall to collect a surprise present for the soon-to-be married couple, Louise and Mark. Your McDonald's type eatery, there were plenty of them around, was quick in producing their choice of food and the three of them settled outside to eat it.

Don was taking others in his car to Canmore, guests to the wedding celebration in four days' time. To relations and guests, Canmore had become a mini holiday for everyone, one resulting in an important occasion at the end of it. The excitement was showing on everyone's faces. The sun was shining, an added bonus to the day and hopefully, the days yet to come.

If the girls expected Canmore to be similar to Edmonton, they were pleasantly surprised. The area was absolutely stunning and picturesque, picture card perfection. A small town with all the comforts required and so eye-catching, wherever you look. Set with the dual carriageway in the distance one side and the hills and mountains on the other side, it was a tranquil place with a beautiful ambience about it. It had ticked all the boxes before they had even gotten out of the car.

The sun shining from above added to the excitement and both Jackie and Claire were ready to explore further, more than ready. The excitement was infectious, both girls' smiles confirmed it. They were raring to go! Canada was so much more than they had ever envisaged in their heads and everything seen so far was totally awe-inspiring. Nectar from the Gods, perhaps!

Claire's eyes lit up when Louise and Mark pulled up alongside Frankie's car. Opening the boot, Mark pulled out Claire's suitcase and handed it to her. Calling into the airport before proceeding their journey to Canmore, Mark had been messaged earlier that morning informing him that the disappearing suitcase had indeed been found.

All of Claire's Christmas came at once. She was over the moon, beaming from ear to ear. Her possessions were back with her, where they belonged. Winning the football pools would have probably become second best to Jackie's sister at that precise moment in time. Words weren't required where Mark and Claire were concerned, the mandatory hugs being more than adequate, more than enough. The gratitude showed all over Claire's face.

Don took the sisters to their rented apartment for the duration in Canmore, within walking distance from their hotel (when not carrying their suitcases that was). A meet-up had been arranged almost immediately, well, within an hour or so, once they'd disposed of their belongings and freshened up. Directions were given and a name of an eatery, a low-key establishment to fill their bellies after a long day travelling.

They managed to drink a cuppa and shower and change before heading off on foot to meet up yet again. Had they managed to find the meeting place in time? Of course, they hadn't. Had they actually found the establishment at all? Another negative response. Their legs walked and walked, asking people along the way and following their directions.

Sadly, with time passing by quickly and two hungry mouths to feed, they'd given up and stopped at an eatery to fill their stomachs, whilst Claire spoke on the mobile phone to Mark and apologised.

Directions were never something that Jackie was good at, with or without Alan on board. The same could be said for Claire and John, getting lost was par for the course. The sisters had done just that, completely lost the plot and had given up come the end. That said, the meal they had eaten was delicious and had hardly hit the sides of their digestive system whilst eating it. The liquid replenishment had fulfilled their thirst. All was good, very good.

They were just finishing off their drinks when all the family members, along with unknown faces, descended upon them. Flabbergasted and surprised, the party was just about to begin! The establishment was a large place, with adequate space to house a pool table, dart board and plenty of room for bums on seats. It appeared that the evening was far from over.

It was probably nearly midnight when the party of people left to go to their individual hotels and apartments in Canmore and retire for the night. With the hugs all done, Jackie and

Claire headed towards their apartment in complete darkness. Were they going the right way? They had no idea and fingers were crossed that they were heading in the right direction. They weren't, nothing looked familiar at all.

Turning around and walking the other way, still unsure of their location, Jackie's legs were finally giving up on her. She needed a rest and found a tree stump, of all things, to sit on for a while. Claire continued walking, desperate for the bathroom facilities of the apartment. It was heading in the right direction, Jackie knew, recognising the silver train parked on the pavement as a reminder of transport in years gone by.

Resting until her legs would work again, Jackie managed to find the apartment on her own. Claire relieved herself in the bathroom facilities and made a cup of tea for them both in preparation for her sister's arrival. Phew! What a nightmare. Sisters were doing it again! Tomorrow was another day and hopefully, calamities of any nature wouldn't arise. Nothing was guaranteed though, ever.

Jackie and Claire were being optimistic, they both knew and the bed beckoned to them. A few hours' sleep was mandatory and they both headed for the stairs completely shattered but happy. Canmore was going to be an exceptional experience and the remaining days were so looked forward to. Psychic they'd not needed to be, Jackie for one, could feel it in her bones.

Claire was already downstairs when Jackie woke up the next morning. She was sitting on the balcony smoking a cigarette and relishing in catching some of the sunshine falling directly on to the balcony. A ray of heaven was sent down from above to spoil her, a hotter than hot experience descending on her body. She loved the sun, Claire had.

Jackie wanted some of it, too. Putting the kettle on for a cuppa, Claire handed her an empty cup to be replenished. Jackie's sister was never fully awake without at least two cups of tea or coffee, the opposite of Jackie herself, who could walk out of her house in the morning after washing, dressing and brushing her teeth; no breakfast or liquid beverage was necessary. She'd preferred the extra time in bed each morning if being honest. Sisters they were but oh so different.

Claire was still in her pyjamas, as was Jackie, there hadn't been anything planned for the morning. They could relax for a while and revel in the picturesque view directly in front of them. Mountains, greenery and tall trees; stunning hotels across the road that added to the beauty of the area enhancing an already hypnotic part of the globe. Everything appeared so clean, fresh and serene. It was as if time had stood still. Residents of the neighbourhood would never realise that they were so lucky to live there.

Did Jackie really need to go back home? Canada was another world, one that was proving to be better and better after each passing day. It was a huge expanse of countryside turned into a town, or towns, that worked without fear and trouble. Maybe, behind the scenes, there was turmoil of sorts but there was no evidence of it showing immediately, nothing transparent anyway.

Jackie was suddenly blinded by a country that enlightened her, lifted her enthusiasm for life and gave her the energy she'd lost over the years. The holiday and wedding invitation was coming to an end. She would be going back to what? A home that was occupied by one person, just Jackie. A sometimes lonely existence in what now seemed a dark and drab country without the excitement that Canada had illuminated and offered.

The sunshine added to the picture, she'd known. Winter would have visualised a completely different analysis of things. The snow falling in the UK was more than enough for Jackie. She knew that she wouldn't have coped with the months and months of the cold white stuff carpeted throughout the whole of the country there. Canada was as cold as it was hot, depending on the season.

The summer months in Canada were so much better than the equivalent weather in the UK, glorious sunshine day after day after day and clear blue skies continuously. Not a cloud in sight! Rain is minimal in comparison. Jackie resided in Wales, say no more! The pluses still outweighed the negatives, didn't they?

The UK was where Jackie's children and grandchildren were, where she needed to be on a permanent basis. She did not want to miss seeing them grow up, not if she could help it.

Sometimes, things were unavoidable and inevitable she'd known but if possible, grandma would be there for them, in whatever capacity required. Granddad wasn't there anymore, through no fault of his own. They were her priorities for sure, first and foremost.

Canada was a dream and she was exploring that dream, a real journey to enlighten her mood and lift her spirits. To realise the joy of living without her soulmate, Alan, by her side. It worked, Jackie loved every second of it. The experience was coming to an end but the wedding was still yet to come.

The next few days would be something else, a fairytale wedding and yet more sightseeing on the agenda. There was more to Canmore than they had seen so far, much more and exploring the town in all its glory was essential. No stone unturned, as the saying goes; Jackie and Claire's legs would walk a lot farther before the final day of their Canadian adventure had come to an end. That was a certainty.

A telephone call from Mark woke the girls up from the relaxing morning, drinking in the glory of what was known as Canmore. Cups had been replenished several times and energy zapped, they were completely relaxed. They were still in their nightwear when he phoned. They were to meet up in a few hours, if wanted, for an ice-cream. Not any old ice-cream but one from the ice-cream bus nearby, a fifteen minute walk away, he'd said.

It made them wake up, triggered their senses and forced them to shower and dress. They did not have breakfast but Jackie was used to that. Seldom did she eat anything of a morning. A cuppa would suffice and occasionally, not even that. It had all depended on what time she'd arisen that morning and whether anything was on the agenda for the day ahead.

More often than not, one meal a day sufficed; living alone allowed her to choose if and when to partake in food. Not being bothered was usually a good enough reason to miss meals, if she was honest with herself. A good idea? Not really but eating had depended on how Jackie felt at the time. Her nan would have cussed her, with a look only she could convey and she would have been right.

Jackie loved having her grandsons over for the weekend. Being forced to feed their hungry mouths meant that she ate too. It was as easy to prepare food for three as it was for two. Jackie somehow found time to feed the little darlings and enjoyed doing it then. Food for one wasn't exciting, not at all.

She did not starve, far from it. Her figure showed that. As Alan had stated years earlier, "she would never be a size 10 again!" Exercise was required as well as dieting to even expect anything near to it and her mobility issues had cancelled out any chance of an hour glass figure. Not that she ever had one in the first place. Love Island eat your heart out!

Claire, Jackie wasn't certain about, as far as breakfast was concerned, that was. Her two cuppas were crucial, mandatory, but on the food front, she did not recall her always eating anything to mop up the breakfast beverages. Whatever, they wouldn't be eating breakfast today. Ice-cream would be their first intake of food.

With them both ready to find the ice-cream bus, they shut the front door behind them and headed in the direction given, hoping for the best. Jackie had her fingers crossed, secretly praying that they wouldn't get lost. A recurrence of yesterday wasn't something either of them had relished. Jackie's legs had only just recovered.

Luck was on their side and they reached the spot without too much trouble. Frankie and Don were already there, and stood in the queue for the cold dessert. As they joined them, others had followed; faces recalled at the late night eatery, family-related or otherwise. The choice of flavours was immense and all looked mouth-wateringly good. Too many to discount but the girls had to decide on one before reaching the front of the queue.

There was a lot of deliberating going on; it would have been so much easier if only vanilla was available. Back in the day, Mr Whippy sold its delicious vanilla ice-cream with the added complimentary flake to enhance its taste and appearance; there was an extra cost for the chocolate flake, of course. The Mr Whippy is still available today, with its concocted variations alongside it.

The ice-cream van back in the UK had the best of both worlds.

Having purchased their ice-creams, Jackie and Claire found a seat to sit on and savour the tub of colourful dessert. It was heaven to their taste buds, explaining the continuous queue of people there to purchase one flavour or another, one that had seldom gone down. Conversation continued from the evening before for what had seemed ages, nothing being duplicated. There was so much to talk about, so much.

Chapter Sixteen

Arrangements had been made to meet up for a pre-reception get-together that evening with all people known and several others soon to be acquainted with; a rehearsal in all intent purposes. Thankfully, the venue was directly opposite the girls' apartment; they simply required walking across the road. No getting lost, for sure. A definite bonus for them both.

With the rest of the afternoon free, it was time to explore and discover the shops. Window shopping primarily but who could deny the grandchildren a souvenir from their holiday cum wedding invitation experience. It was a reason to pursue the retail area of Canmore, not that they required an excuse to spend.

Holidays were there to see and buy, for necessities sake rather than something avoidable. Pennies saved for the regular breaks from normal living had usually afforded some spending monies on things not really needed but wanted, all the same. Splashing out once in a while, Jackie would have called it.

'I'm worth it,' suddenly filled Jackie's head as she shouted out loudly. A phrase regularly repeated on the television commercials of today. The products, shampoo and hair dyes were being promoted. The brand name escaped her for the time being but it would come back to her eventually. Usually at the most inconvenient time, whilst thinking about something else. Old age doesn't come alone.

With grandchildren of different ages and characters, buying presents for them was never an easy task. What one liked, the other was either too young or too old for something similar. Some were boys and others girls, colours being instrumental in their purchases. Buying pink for a boy wasn't a usual occurrence.

Jackie would disagree where her middle grandson was concerned. At seven years of age, his favourite colour was still pink. A boy with a caring nature who loved and played with the girls rather than the boys in school, Jackie and her family had given him what he wanted. A bright pink flamingo back pack to carry his schoolwork and lunch-box in was his choice and he carried it with pride.

Whilst most boys had the black or dark blue equivalent, he was destined to be different, as all children are. Jackie and Claire loved all of their grandchildren with a passion; one not to be beaten. Devils or angels, they were the adults of the future generation with unique personalities; all inheriting something of their grandparents' nature, good or bad. Were there more to come in the future? Who could tell?

Dressing for the occasion was similar to getting ready for the future wedding. Both girls wanted to look nice; there were new people to meet and interact with, after all. Claire now owned several dress choices. A ladies' prerogative, perhaps. After purchasing two dresses in Canada for the wedding celebration, her suitcase had been recovered, along with the original outfit bought back in the UK.

She deliberated before making her final decision; Canada's clothing outlets were filled with dresses galore, several suiting the older women, a definite plus for Claire (and Jackie for that matter). It was one of her newest purchases that she'd worn, along with her black "comfy" heels.

The word "comfy" wasn't something that Jackie would have included in the sentence, though. Jackie's dress was okay as fashion had gone. Nothing fancy but a style that suited her humble figure. Flat shoes it had to be. Anything with a heel as far as footwear was concerned was out of the equation. A nightmare waiting to happen, Jackie would have called it. No way, Jose!

Time had passed since wearing the stiletto heel was a normality, years in fact. Claire's sister couldn't walk in them anymore and had abandoned her love of the delicate and slimming footwear of her teens through to her forties. How Jackie envied her sister for being able to wear them.

Heels always did a posh dress justice, adding class to an outfit.

A few items of jewellery and a hint of make-up, both were ready to join in yet another evening out. Jackie was going to miss all the meals out when back home alone, she knew. Spoilt she'd been, without a doubt. As they walked across the road from their apartment, gazing at the fabulous views in front of them, smiles adorned their faces, for sure. It was a privilege to be alive.

Jackie thought about Alan, suddenly. He would have loved being there with them, revelling in the atmosphere of Canada and its beauty, along with the glorious wall-to-wall sunshine. Hopefully, heaven was as beautiful. Jackie so wanted him to be happy, whatever he was doing there. Idle hands were never in Alan's nature, he had to be doing something, hadn't he?

As expected, the evening was a roaring success. The food was delicious, mouth-wateringly so, with way too much choice. Roast beef and Yorkshire pudding with all the trimmings was on the menu, along with several desserts including apple crumble and custard, a firm favourite among the guests there. Canadians loved the English favourites as much as the British people did.

Jackie had never been able to eat stewed apples of any description. In a pie, crumble or baked with sultanas, her stomach would heave just looking at it. Some Danish pastries had hidden apple slices inside and Claire's sister would be running to the toilet spitting it out, before being physically sick. Her body had a grudge against anything relating to stewed apples, it had appeared, from a very young age.

Alan had loved the apple desserts, so Jackie would serve them to him regularly, after a main meal; washing the dirty dishes up afterwards had her stomach churning. The smell of the stewed apple causing untold messages to her brain. She'd hated doing it but had persevered over the years.

Love had a lot to answer for!

Rhubarb crumble was a compromise, the produce grown in the garden. All the family would eat it with creamy custard, Jackie included. A pudding with definite advantages, the body ridding itself of unwanted impurities along with a sometimes hasty visit to the toilet. A must for those with constipation, all good there.

Filling the large plate given to her with the roast beef lunch, there was little room left for a dessert so Jackie abstained from the second course. The wine was flowing freely and conversation continued throughout the evening, all in a very positive way. Newfound friends and acquaintances were illuminated with living in the UK, interested in all that was English, Welsh, Scottish and Irish. Claire and Jackie were both happy to oblige.

The hours passed quickly and guests headed for home, or their hotels or apartments, whichever had fitted. Walking back to their apartment, the girls managed a cup of tea before heading up the stairs to bed. With sleeping usually a problem for Jackie, Canada was proving otherwise for her. It hadn't taken long to enter the land of nod.

There were just two days left in Canada and the wedding day came at last. Mark and Louise gave instructions as to when to arrive at the hotel where they were staying. A minibus would be on hand to transport them to the wedding venue, a hilltop golf course with several buildings housing functions and entertainment, there with facilities of all sorts.

The weather was gorgeous; a sunny day devoid of any clouds spoiling the clear blue sky above. Just what the doctor had ordered. Perfection itself. Who could ask for anything more? The angels above were shining down on the couple in question, for certain. God had wanted a day to remember for them.

It was an afternoon ceremony but the girls were asked to be at the hotel for eleven o'clock in the morning. Tradition or not, Canada they were in, guests were instructed to follow the groom through the hotel's grounds. A groom who had his back turned away from the love of his life's arrival shortly afterwards. Watching from the garden above, Louise tapped Mark's shoulder, indicating her presence and he was allowed to turn around and see his bride.

She looked beautiful in her wedding dress, an outfit befitting her and adding to her pretty features. Mark looked good too but eyes were all on the bride, as always. Louise looked radiant, glowing with excitement, the happiness showing through. If she was nervous at all, it hadn't shown.

The day had only just begun but was going to be a day to remember, for all the right reasons. Love was definitely in the air. Couples were there, smiling; beaming from ear to ear remembering their own wedding day, whenever that was or looking forward to their own unique ceremony to come. Time was immaterial and the memories were enlightened between guests, old and young. Jackie recalled her own wedding.

Not so luxurious or fairytale-like as Mark and Louise's but equally as memorable. She so missed Alan and now, at that moment in time, it became relevant. He wasn't there to escort her to the celebration that was yet to come, a glorious occasion to revel in and smile about. Marriages were a joyous occasion and so uplifting. A heart-rending experience, for sure.

A "normal" church wedding followed by a reception above the public house opposite Melinda's family home and the evening get-together there directly afterwards. Melinda was one of five siblings, as was Peter; the number of seats on bums at the reception was a good number to start with. That was before adding Melinda's aunties and uncles and her nan; Thomas was the baby of thirteen children so the addition of more bums on seats hadn't included cousins or well-loved friends of either family.

The guest list needed to stop somewhere, finances permitting.

That wasn't to say that their presence wasn't appreciated at the evening get-together, it was; Melinda's direct family descendants were of a huge proportion and she'd recalled a "garage" get-together for her nan's ninetieth birthday. There wasn't a venue big enough to take all who had attended; children, grandchildren and great-grandchildren had wanted to be there, so her uncle's garage and the large garden incorporated in the property had sufficed.

Nevertheless, Melinda was grateful for all her relatives, mostly all in contact with Thomas, Amelia and the children on a regular basis.

To Melinda, family was so important. More so that being money-rich; grandparents, parents and siblings had outdone anything orientated by financial collateral, though having enough funds to pay the bills on time was something required in today's world, for definite. Holidays were crucial to a year's worth of living, in Melinda's eyes, something well worth saving up for. A family break was a few days to behold and so so enjoyed for everything it represented.

Melinda and Peter's wedding had included everything that was wanted; neither of them was disappointed. The vicar had stood on the church wall taking photographs of the occasion, full of excitement. Not something expected from a member of the cloth. He revelled in the occasion along with every other person there. All good, bringing back memories to cherish forever.

Climbing into the minibus, heading towards the wedding venue, Jackie well understood the choice of location. It was absolutely stunning and awe-inspiring, the view from the minibus alone was breathtaking. Open-mouthed the sisters were, just seeing the spectacular sights in front of them passing by. What must it be like at the very top, they had wondered? They were soon to find out.

As they dismounted the minibus, the girls followed the crowd. They were all going to the same place, weren't they? There in front of them was an outdoor semblance of furniture, purposely situated where the wedding ceremony was to be held. Jackie had only ever seen it in the movies. A television film of a romantic nature, with a happy ending usually of a wedding between the two lovebirds, an outdoor one at that.

Jackie was gobsmacked, all in a good way. The scene was stunning, to die for, with views of the mountains ahead staring them in the face. Had they gone to heaven? It was a fairytale, at least. Recalling Alan's proposal whilst visiting Las Vegas a few years back; he'd wanted their wedding vows renewed there. She'd turned her nose up at the suggestion, remarking that she'd already done it once. Now, on seeing the beautiful creation in front of her, she was regretting the refusal; especially with Alan no longer being here.

Chairs were set on both sides of the aisle, all uniform and precise. Ahead was the decorated spot, where Mark and Louise were to be married, becoming a couple, man and wife. Flowers had adorned the area, beautifully put together with colours reminiscent of a happy occasion yet to happen. A wedding, in fact. Flowers and a marriage knitted together perfectly. There wasn't a sad face amongst any of the guests. A rare occurrence in this day and age.

Chapter Seventeen

Contrary to tradition, the photographer had taken group photos of the guests, including the bride and groom, before the actual ceremony. A tad strange but a request from Mark and Louise, as it happened. All made complete sense, giving added time to celebrate the couple's union, after the event. A note for others, perhaps.

On the negative side, if they decided to not go ahead with the wedding nuptials then the photographs would have been wasted. That wasn't going to happen unless one of them had a secret hidden in their closet. Had they? Of course, they hadn't, they both adored each other. Two beings meant to be together, forever. The signs were all there for everyone to see. Love was definitely in the air and the day couldn't have been better; not a cloud in the sky.

Sunshine and awesome scenery were always preferential to dark and gloomy days, enhancing the spirit, the mind and mental well-being. The proof was there, excitement on everyone's faces. A day to remember for all the right reasons. Today was a good day, a brilliant one and something to celebrate and recall. Memories to cherish and treasure until old and weary, most definitely. A wedding was something to blow away the cobwebs, to relish in the glory of uniting two people so much in love.

A match made in heaven, to be delighted in, whilst on earth. A linking of two souls and living as man and wife for the rest of their lives, or the foreseeable years to come, at best. No one could predict the future.

Mark had met his wife-to-be in Wales, UK and their attraction to each other was instantaneous.

Louise, a Canadian, remained in the UK for years, with periodical returns to her home country. Both living together whilst studying for their chosen careers, she'd returned to Canada and her hometown only for Mark to follow her and make Louise's birthplace his home, too.

Their relationship was meant to be, no doubt about it. The writing was on the wall, as the saying goes. They were destined to be together. Countries apart hadn't deterred the final outcome as a lot of relationships had in the past. Mark and Louise's fate was already mapped out and miles and miles apart, the love had stood its stead.

Jackie couldn't have said the same on meeting Alan if she was honest. She hadn't liked him at all. The feelings weren't reciprocated though, thankfully. Alan would turn up, like a sore thumb at times, whenever she turned her back. He would phone her once a week, asking the same question and getting the same negative answer, 'No.' Eventually, Jackie gave in to a first date and the rest is history.

It was a laughable experience now, proving that things weren't always as clear-cut. Love at first sight wasn't something that every married couple had witnessed. Forty-three years of marriage had shown their love and commitment to one another, though. The love had grown over the years and

Alan was so missed today. He was her soulmate. His presence would have sealed Jackie's elation to Mark and Louise's celebration. It wasn't meant to be, that's life.

Nothing is ever mapped out, sadly. Canadian traditions were somewhat confusing. The run-up to the actual wedding ceremony had lasted ages, so much longer than that in the UK. Different, would probably be the right word to describe it, totally different but unique. Not wrong at all, not every wedding service was destined to be identical. That would be so boring.

UK tradition had the bride and groom not meeting face to face until they had reached the presence of the vicar or whoever was performing the wedding service, the binding of two souls. Superstition was a funny thing and it was supposed to be bad luck when seeing the bride on the day of her committal, before the actual ceremony. It was entirely up to the individual whether to believe in the superstition or not.

The groom would usually first see his future wife as she walked down the aisle with her father or a family member. There to give her away, perhaps reluctantly. A happy occasion with the bride being transferred from one family member to her soon-to-be spouse. A joyous occasion, with a hint of sadness on losing the bride-to-be from her immediate family; only temporarily though.

Life's predictions, marriage was, for the majority of people; as things seemed. The lucky ones, one might think but that was a matter of choice today. Not everybody's cup of tea, as they say! Thank goodness everybody wasn't the same and had individual goals for their future. The world would be a sorry state of affairs, otherwise.

Eventually, everyone was seated in their designated space in preparation for the upcoming nuptials; the whole reason they were there. Everything was planned out meticulously. There was no room for error. The day had to be perfect, with no exceptions. The planning had been thoroughly thought out. Nothing was going to spoil it and nothing did.

With both Mark and Louise stood in pride of place taking their vows, the bridesmaids and smartly suited out gentlemen there all stood still in front of them, facing the besotted pair as they spoke lovingly to one another. The witnesses were there, every single guest hearing the words spoken by both Mark and Louise. The words "I do" being so important.

The rings, wedding bands and the mandatory kiss completed, the service and the married couple moved to a table nearby to sign the necessary document declaring them as an official couple. A round of applause from everyone occurred as they signed on the dotted line, both willingly. Mr and Mrs they now were and a whole new chapter of their lives was about to begin. Radiance had shone throughout every person there, willing the newlyweds a future filled with everything good.

Unknowingly, the two sisters, Jackie and Claire, suddenly became popular people. The Canadian guests wanted to speak to the visitors from the UK, Jackie and Claire being just two of them. Introductions from various relatives had conversations galore about everything and nothing. The UK was a place on the world map that the Canadians had wanted to know a lot about.

Both sisters filled them in on anything they required to know, if they indeed knew themselves. Looking around Canada, to Jackie at least, the UK was so drab and uneventful in comparison; but not to them. Jackie, for one, was surprised. The Canadians had so much more beauty around them and she envied them their existence there.

Who couldn't wake up on a morning and drink in the fabulous scenery radiating from every angle around? Dark and damp corners were something Jackie registered in her head of her birthplace. She must have been looking somewhere else, mustn't she? Bristol, UK had never been pretty, a city it was at the end of the day. Historic, maybe but pretty, no.

Wales, in all fairness, was a green valley and so much nicer. It rained there a lot. The hills and dales were not in Canada's league at all, unique as they were to the UK. Neither Jackie nor Claire could understand the interest or the questions relating to their birthplace, along with the excitement when asking. They did their best to satisfy their curiosity, in their knowledge of their own country, the UK.

Fish and chips eaten from the wrapper was what the UK was famous for, wasn't it? There was something else the UK was notorious for; something the natives of Canada had taken to their hearts and adopted as their own, well tried any roads. As the guests had entered the reception area, resplendent with huge tables, chairs (some that had decided, against all odds, to break upon being seated) and flowers in abundance, that something had raised its head once again, on the sisters' recent travels.

The English Sunday roast was being served. Roast beef and Yorkshire pudding with all the trimmings; vegetables galore and thick brown gravy as an accompaniment. A simple meal, yet one loved for just that, being simple. Meat and fresh vegetables served on a large dinner plate before adding the thick runny liquid. Horseradish sauce was served with it, a matter of taste for most. Absolute heaven and the Canadians' favourite, apparently.

Jackie then realised that her birthplace had something else to offer, besides the fish and chip suppers. Apple crumble and thick creamy custard for dessert, not something Jackie could eat but Canada's obsession with the dessert was equally hypnotic. The UK and its food variations had obviously become a hit and Jackie smiled to herself proudly.

With the wine flowing amidst speeches from various family members and friends of the newlyweds, Jackie's head began to feel disorientated, a little light-headed, tipsy even. Not a drinker of alcohol, as a rule, just two glasses of wine had suddenly gone to her head, almost immediately.

Perhaps, the hot sunshine had something to do with it as well.

Not liking how she was feeling, she abstained from alcohol for the remainder of the day. Only drinking water seemed a tad drastic but Jackie knew that it was the only way forward. A party pooper she wasn't (well, not on this occasion) and wanted to let her hair down on the wedding event. Eating the roast beef and Yorkshire pudding meal with a dizzy and spaced-out image of her food, Jackie did what was needed and kept her brain sensible and in focus.

Claire's sister needed to be aware of her actions throughout the remainder of the day, the afternoon and the evening ahead. Dull as dishwater, Jackie would describe herself but better that than making a complete fool of herself. The limelight hadn't suited Jackie at all. A wallflower was much more favourable, in keeping with how she was foreseen by others.

Had Claire and the other occupants of the table at the reception that Jackie had been seated at noticed her hazy head struggling to eat her food? Had they wondered why she was babbling on about things without taking a breather? Conversation it was called but Jackie, in all honesty, was trying to eradicate the lost vision from her eyes. All she was seeing was a cloudy image in front of her, something she did not like at all.

As the waiter offered more wine or water at their table, Jackie immediately opted for the alcohol-free option. What volume of alcohol had been in those two glasses of wine she drank? The liquid had hit parts of her brain she'd not used before, well, not for a long time anyway. As she'd finished her main course, having refused the apple crumble and custard dessert or any other type of sweet confectionery, some air was required and she'd gotten up from the chair and headed towards the outdoors.

Hoping that the fresh air would help to eradicate the dizziness, Jackie kept quiet about the disorientation she felt and the reason behind it. No one needed to know, did they? If Claire's sister felt a fool before then, today was another date to add to her list. What would Alan have thought, Jackie wondered looking towards the clear blue sky.

The grounds around the wedding venue were nothing short of spectacular. There was no other word that could describe it. With the added brilliant sunshine, it was a picture postcard extravaganza. The phones were clicking all around, at all angles of the area, bringing guests into group photos and including Jackie and Claire into them.

Both girls took photos for guests of the wedding party, including the camera or phone owner in the picture. Courtesy at its best. Amelia and Thomas, their parents, had taught their children to be polite and helpful, something that had cost absolutely nothing to the young children then.

A golf course was part of the establishment, and although no one was seen using it on the day, the buggies were driven around the large expanse of land. Today, they escorted wedding guests from the reception area to the ceremonial platform and back again; saving their legs climbing up and down a sometimes steep incline. Jackie was eternally grateful for the lift, struggling to manage the terrain with her mobility issues. Claire was on hand to hold her steady but better to be safe than sorry. A phrase oh so true. Falling flat on her face, Jackie hadn't wanted.

Jackie had been transported from the area that the happy couple had taken their vows, to the reception area just as two deer approached the outside of the venue; she could almost touch them. Managing to take a quick photo, she was well pleased. The buggy driver had forewarned her of the animals evident around the corner.

Jackie was well prepared and thanked him for the ride and the experience. She'd never been that close to a deer before and probably never would again in the future. Canada was still ticking all the boxes, even now.

With the food eaten and the majority of the guests now outside drinking up the fabulous views and an atmosphere filled with elation and pure excitement, the girls walked and investigated more of the resort, intrigued by what else was there to be seen. Walking off the light-headedness was another reason, as far as Jackie was concerned. Her legs were a tad unsteady and she'd hidden it well, very well.

Two buggies drove past and Jackie shouted out to the driver of one of them, 'Can I have a lift?' Why, she'd no clue, the alcohol had obviously gotten the better of her. A sober Jackie wouldn't have done that, for certain. Shouting out to a complete stranger wasn't what Claire's sister was about. She was far too shy for that.

The buggy driver stopped and spoke to them both, asking where they wanted to go and offering them a ride. Jackie conveyed that she was only joking before turning a brighter shade of red and feeling embarrassed. What was she like? A conversation erupted between the three of them for a good while afterwards.

A young lad he was, not a sixty-something adult and Jackie, for one, was surprised at the easy conversation that had emerged as a result of her outburst. A Canadian lad conversing with two "elderly" English ladies as if they'd known each other for ages. Waving goodbye to him, he had gone on his way, to wherever he was heading around the grounds of the establishment. Happy as Larry sprung to mind and Jackie was feeling calm and contented, stress-free for a change.

Claire was too, they were both thoroughly taken up with the day's events.

A memory to be instilled in the sisters' heads forever, one from across the pond and all that the country (Canada) had to give; it had a lot to give, so much to take in and devour. Both Jackie and Claire had been well and truly spoilt. Nothing dampened the experience, absolutely nothing. A chance in a lifetime it had been, for both girls and one that would remain foremost in their minds for a long time to come.

The wedding was indeed the icing on the cake and an ending to Claire and Jackie's journey that couldn't be repeated, well not in a long time any roads.

Chapter Eighteen

With the food cleared away, except for a table filled with "nibbles" for guests to partake in when passing by, small individual cakes and biscuits of all descriptions, looked so mouth-watering and utterly delicious. After a hearty meal consisting of mainly meat and vegetables, along with apple crumble and thick creamy custard, the majority of guests were full to bursting and at the time couldn't eat another morsel of food. Needing to undo a button or two was more to the point.

Delicious food requires exercise to fully digest the contents and feel more comfortable in their clothing. It had been time to bring on the music and discover the dance floor, for guests to show off their steps, and their moves and delight in the rest of the evening. Bopping to the beat of the song and strutting their stuff, nothing was uniform where the dancing was concerned.

People were unique and so was their style of dance to the tunes playing from the disco, complete with colourful lighting creating an ambience in the large reception room.

Not everyone would be joining in with the moves on the dance floor, Jackie being one of them. Claire abstained as well but, unlike Jackie, was a good dancer. Alan would have vouched for that; Claire and Alan's moves to the 1960s/1970s popular tunes of the day were a joy to watch way back then. Elvis Presley and Jerry Lee Lewis certainly knew how to create a dance audience. Jackie's reasoning, due to mobility issues today, wasn't an excuse to remain seated.

She couldn't dance when younger, having two left feet and no rhythm in her hips whatsoever. Nothing had changed on that score, stiff as cardboard Jackie's attempt at dancing was then and still is today. The chances of her performing on the dance floor now weren't negotiable. Leaving those able to move to the music was admirable.

The guests were truly enjoying themselves and the girls watched and smiled. The party was well into full swing as Mark and Louise hoped for. All was good and the evening was far from over. The night was still young as people might say. The alcoholic bar was now open to those who wanted to replenish their glasses and Jackie remained on the non-alcoholic version, pure water with added ice (more water).

As the evening continued, more food was brought out to the side table, now almost emptied of the sweet delicacies. Popping a biscuit or cake into one's mouth as they passed the dance floor had worked a treat. In its place now was a table laden with pizzas, several different variations to choose from. Both girls abstained from any more food but others had tucked in, food to mop up the alcohol perhaps!

Midnight turned into one o'clock the next morning and although the guests were slowly dwindling and leaving for home, or their hotels and apartments, staying until the end was Claire's preference. Jackie was tired, admittedly but knowing that it would be a long time before seeing the family again, in Jackie's case maybe never, it made complete sense. Canada wasn't just down the road.

Mark and Louise had supplied minibuses to escort guests to wherever they had wanted to go, after the day and evening celebrations had concluded. Frankie had been informed by the staff there that the flowers supplied by her for the occasion would be disposed of in the bin the following morning. If she or anyone else wanted to take any of the said flowers home with them, they would be welcome to take as many as they could carry.

Claire hadn't wanted to see the displays binned and picked up a reasonably sized bouquet as both the girls headed for one of the minibuses situated just outside the venue. Today was their last day in Canada and sadly, they would be heading for the airport the next morning, ready to fly back to the UK in the afternoon.

What Claire was going to do with the flowers had Jackie wondering. Maybe she was going to leave them in the apartment, ready for the next occupants. Whatever, Claire's reasoning had been a good one. Leaving them there to be dumped into a heap in the outside bin was devastating, barbaric even.

The preparation to detail and the gorgeous colouring of the flowers in season were well too good to be abandoned when some good could have come of them. If there had been a churchyard nearby, they could have brightened up the gravestones, bringing a little light to the occupants no longer in this world. Definitely better than discarding the blooms completely.

With the minibus full, the driver asked everyone's location and dropped each and every person to their designated place. Claire then asked the driver if he was married and he replied positively. Handing the bouquet to him, she told him to give it to his wife. He was well pleased and thanked her. Once again, Amelia and Thomas' upbringing reared its head. Politeness and generosity cost nothing and the gesture was spot on. A happy smile adorned the driver's face. Good one, Claire.

A few hours' sleep was needed but not before a cup of tea nightcap. If the girls thought that the wedding day was the last time that they would see the family, then they were sadly mistaken. Both Jackie and Claire were to meet the newlyweds and Louise's parents and siblings, including their spouses and children at the hotel for an after wedding breakfast.

A new one to the girls, not something traditional on the UK menu. Knowing that shortly afterwards, a taxi would be taking them to Calgary airport for their journey home, that few hours' sleep was recommended. Both climbing the stairs to their bedrooms, and neither of them needed any rocking.

Jackie, as organised as ever, managed to pack her suitcase the morning before the wedding ceremony, only leaving out clothing items that were needed for the wedding day itself and the following morning. Rushing around last minute wasn't something she liked, even though at times there was no choice in the matter. A headless chicken came to mind, flapping around all over the place and getting nowhere. Jackie would have forgotten something, she'd been certain. Better to be prepared. Organisation was Jackie's middle name, as a rule.

With having to vacate the apartment by a certain time, pulling the suitcases and hand luggage from there to the hotel for the breakfast date was doable and they'd taken their time, avoiding any accidents along the way. Mark was there to meet them in the foyer and took their belongings to his hotel room for safekeeping.

The taxi was to pick them up from the hotel and transport them to Calgary airport for the ensuing departure to their homeland, the UK. Jackie, for one, didn't want to leave; she could have willingly stayed a while longer. A family home, occupied by just one solitary person wasn't all it was cracked up to be; Jackie knew so well.

Plans were mapped out and inevitable, the girls would be saying goodbye soon and both being a tad tearful was expected. The experience had been everything and more than anticipated. A few weeks out of a normal daily routine was something that everyone should do, once in a while. Similar to famous brands of breakfast tea, it made everything better. Tea is the elixir of life and an answer to most of their problems.

A break away from the norm had the same effect and educated their minds. All good as things had turned out. Age was immaterial where learning was concerned and both sisters learnt a lot on their trip to Canada. Whether the information had sunk in for future reference was unknown and debatable; Jackie's forgetfulness had increased over the years. She couldn't speak for Claire; she was the younger of the two of them.

As they both entered the dining area of the hotel, they had no illusions as to the amount of variations on the breakfast menu and they did not need to be psychic. Full English breakfast aside, the continental section excelled itself. The cereal selection was equally as impressive. Jackie, as a rule at home, missed the breakfast meal, usually due to getting up too late in the morning. There was a logical reason for continuing the lie-in, so to speak.

A sole occupier of her house, she'd only herself to think about. It made her a tad lazy if she was honest. Why bother to polish and dust every day when it was only her seeing it? She ensured the house was tidy but everyday dusting, etc., wasn't required and mobility issues aside, she had too much time on her hands as a result. Getting up late was a woman's prerogative, wasn't it? Being retired was another excuse for a duvet day, as Jackie saw it.

The grandsons gave her things to do, generally at their abode. When babysitting at Jackie's, it inevitably gave her some extra housework to do and she did not mind at all; cleaning for cleaning's sake wasn't in Jackie's list of "to-dos" though and she stuck to it.

Stood in the queue to decide on what to eat that morning had her in a quandary. Knowing they would have a long journey ahead of them, she needed to eat something substantial. The mandatory cups of tea were essential, she knew; food also required digesting and Jackie's head recognised the need for solid substance. She plated the equivalent of an English breakfast out, minus the baked beans (she liked them but had preferred tinned spaghetti) and had carried the contents to a vacant table.

Claire had done the same. Sensible, the sisters were when required to be. Conversation between Mark, Louise and the family had continued throughout the breakfast meal; all persons present appeared wide awake and eager to devour the day ahead. With the amount of alcohol consumed the evening before, nobody there looked any worse for wear. Jackie, for one, was pleasantly surprised. After just two glasses of wine, she'd abstained from alcohol for the rest of the evening; reluctantly but sensibly.

Just the thought of her being drunk and disorderly was enough to commit to water but a few more alcoholic beverages would have been nice. Jackie would have put herself in an entirely different position and had all there talking about her, she knew, as a result. A room full of clear heads and Jackie, she could see it all in front of her, vividly. Would she have behaved on the wedding evening? Wetting the newlyweds' heads would have willingly taken centre stage, in the scheme of things. It wasn't to be, sadly.

Breakfast had gone on for absolutely ages, long enough to eat and drink plenty and speak to everyone there twice over. With Mark bringing their luggage down from his and Louise's room in the hotel, realised the time and the arrival of the taxi and its driver; there to take Jackie and Claire to the airport.

Hugs were exchanged as they got into the taxi. Jackie's emotions were getting the better of her and she hid her face from the Canadian residents waving to the girls. Unbeknown to them both, they were all tearful too. An experience of a lifetime was coming to an end, one that had reached the parts of the sisters' minds that other holidays hadn't done in a long long time. Tired they may have been but Jackie wouldn't have missed out on the adventure or the highlights of the holiday itself.

Ever grateful for the wedding invitation, Jackie would be, until the end of her days. A vacation that would be talked about and recalled throughout the remainder of the sisters' lives. Life was meant for living, wasn't it? A white feather suddenly dropped from the skies above to the ground below, landing directly in front of them as Chester had driven away. Alan had given his approval and a tear dropped from Jackie's eye.

As busy as it was at Calgary airport with bodies everywhere, rushing about all over the place, the girls managed to find the check-out easily enough. Claire had concerns over the weight of the personal belongings in her suitcase, so Jackie was able to move some of the contents into her own baggage carrier.

Having purchased several clothing items during the Canada experience, the excess baggage could have been expensive. No more additional costs were required; Claire would need to have claimed the extra expense back from either the insurance policy purchased or the airline itself when back home. Something that would have probably been a lengthy ordeal in itself.

Ever grateful for getting them back, dealing with the paperwork was taken as it was; better to get her loved belongings back than lose them completely. If the situation had been reversed and Jackie had been the one losing her belongings, truthfully, she'd have been beside herself with worry. Her lucky mascot, a repaired ceramic piskie, had travelled everywhere she had gone when away from home.

Broken by dropping it when emptying her suitcase, Jackie lovingly superglued it together and she continued to take it on her travels. It was a well-travelled piskie, for sure! Superstition at its best, the Cornish piskie was an ugly thing but to Jackie, represented safety when travelling and was supposed to be lucky.

Alan had taken her to Padstow, Cornwall, one year, after she'd broken it. Jackie found the piskie shop by chance and purchased a replacement. So excited, Alan had merely smiled and nodded, whilst resting in the car for her to hunt out the famous piskie shop. The new one had resided in the Welsh dresser in her living room now. Her trusted original travelled with her always, still. Jackie would have been upset if she'd lost the ceramic object, something completely worthless to anyone else.

Recalling another holiday, one where she lovingly wrapped her piskie in a scarf and put it into her hand luggage, Jackie smiled to herself and giggled loudly. She could see it all now, as if it had happened yesterday. The staff member had checked goods on the conveyor belt, items scanned as they'd reached her. She had then asked Jackie to remove the hand luggage contents. Unwrapping the piskie very carefully, her face was expressionless and surprised.

She indicated for Jackie to proceed to the departure lounge in readiness for their journey abroad, saying nothing else at all. Alan's face had been a picture, seeing him there in front of her so clearly. Residing in the luggage container from now on was compulsory. Jackie would never live it down again, for certain. The blushes would be very evident and explanations as to the piskie's reason for being there, laughable. At sixty-six years of age, it was no wonder.

Costa Coffee was eagerly sought out; Claire was in urgent need of the mandatory liquid drink before boarding the plane. Thankfully, it was a direct flight and once bums were settled in their designated seats, they could both relax and sleep, whichever suited. Jackie was praying to herself that Claire wouldn't pass out again as the plane headed for the skies above.

Her prayers were answered and Jackie's sister was fine, well she looked it anyway. Her heart was probably racing with the fear but she was there nevertheless, sat beside her sister.

Chapter Nineteen

The drive back from Heathrow was as turbulent as the plane journey itself. Jackie's fear of motorway driving was always filled with trepidation; panicking all the while with the quick succession of cars and lorries overtaking and shifting from lane to lane to lane. Jackie had hated it and suffered them very rarely. On this occasion, she couldn't get out of it.

The chance of getting lost after entering the wrong lane and unable to manoeuvre out of it without causing an accident was always there in the back of her mind. Jackie and directions were and always would be a nightmare; getting lost when not aware of recognised locations was a frequent occurrence. An avid driver, Claire's sister wasn't. Being behind the wheel was done out of necessity rather than a pleasurable experience. The nerves would always be evident on any journey, long or short.

Usually, she would take the National Express Coach to Claire and John's, ditching the car for a lengthy but hassle-free ride was definitely preferable. Sadly, on this occasion, she had no choice in the matter. The focus on the road halted the conversation with Claire, needing to fully interact with the job at hand, getting them back from Gatwick to Claire and

John's residence in one piece. A goal requiring complete and utter concentration on Jackie's part.

A few stops along the way were mandatory, just to ease Jackie's head and body of the imminent concerns to hand. Costa Coffee, or the equivalent, was found as well as the much-needed break from the motorway driving, along with the toilet requirements. Coffee had needed to be let out, too. The phrase "getting a dog to learn new tricks" had suddenly come to mind whilst seated in the cafe.

Try as she might, Jackie had always detested driving, where three or more lanes were evident.

Claire's sister couldn't be taught to like the experience and preferred abstinence over trial. Stubborn maybe, Jackie had known her limitations. Where was Alan when she needed him the most? A silent tear had dropped from an eye. He was missed so much by both sisters.

Eventually, they reached Bristol and Jackie let out a huge sigh of relief. Mentally exhausted, she remained in the car for ages; stuck to her seat it appeared. In a somewhat daze, a world of her own, a voice echoed loudly in her brain. Looking around, John stood there, knocking on the window. Surprised, Jackie smiled up at him. Claire was already outside, lifting the luggage from the boot.

Pleased with herself, Jackie moved, opening the door to a sisterly hug from John; a much-needed one. She had done it, she wanted to shout out to all who could hear her but decided against it. Jackie had only driven from Gatwick to Bristol, not landed on the moon! An everyday occurrence for many, no big deal in reality. But it was for Claire's sister, an achievement not for the faint-hearted or particularly for those with a fear of motorways.

Who exactly feared motorways? Jackie asked the question silently.

Jackie had, for one. Was she in the minority? Probably she was; nevertheless, she'd achieved the unachievable. Would she want to do it again? Not in a hurry but never say never. Choice wouldn't take her there; sometimes there was no other alternative in the matter. Life was life, circumstances could force the issue, accepting the inevitable.

With the luggage now in the house, or bungalow as it had happened, a cup of tea was urgently required. A congratulatory drink after a long drive, after a long flight from Canada, no less. Were the sisters tired? It hadn't shown if they were. John was pleased to see Claire back home, he'd missed her. Jackie was part of the family package; like it or not, she was there like a sore thumb. Thankfully, not a pain in the backside. It hadn't been implied anyway!

Living independently and alone, there were probably a few habits that Jackie inherited from somewhere or someone around. Stubbornness would be one of her worst attributes since losing Alan and Jackie would openly admit to it. Asking for help was something she tried not to do unless it was absolutely necessary, essential in fact. Would there be a positive solution if she'd spoken up? Sometimes, Jackie was her own worst enemy.

Amelia, Jackie's mum, had been the same as she aged and Jackie's angry words to her mum for not asking for help were frequent conversations until her death at eighty-two years of age. Like mother, like daughter. Jackie was replicating her mum often and knew it. A chip off the old block maybe.

Alan wasn't there to have a go at, was he? As a married couple, words had been uttered over the years; some arguments along the way were par for the course. It wouldn't have been healthy to never disagree throughout their relationship. Characteristics aside though, they were a compatible match and had lasted the course. Alan should have welcomed the girls back from Canada but it was John, alone, who was there to greet them. He was so missed, for sure.

Jackie was staying at John and Claire's for a few days before returning to Wales and her home. Extending the holiday even further was something she did not mind at all. Claire was going back to work in two days' time, so spending time in their home was good. John, after asking about their adventures, and their vacation, handed them both a take-away menu and they both deliberated as to what to eat. They were both being spoilt rotten. The holiday hadn't ended just yet.

Claire unpacked her suitcase of her dirty laundry and was filling the washing machine up as Jackie made yet another cup of tea. The nectar of the Gods was something that Jackie couldn't get enough of. Much more preferable to addictive wine from Canada; she giggled to herself as the kettle boiled, just thinking about it.

Both girls were shattered after their journey from Canada, via taxi, plane and car; it was only when they were settled in front of the television that the exhaustion actually hit them both. An early night was recommended and John was more than happy with their decision. The beds were waiting for them, calling to them, early as the evening was.

With Claire not starting back to work the following day, neither Claire nor Jackie had required getting up early the following morning, unlike John; something they were both more than grateful for. A lie-in was being looked forward to. Canada's itinerary included numerous early morning calls and

Jackie's regular getting up time hadn't included an early rise from bed, as a rule. Claire's work routine, on the other hand, was the exact opposite and she was used to hearing the birds calling to her most mornings.

Jackie had no idea as to what time Claire arose from her extended sleep the next morning. A knock on Jackie's bedroom door had her jolting from a very deep sleep, something rare (very rare) for her. Claire's 'Are you awake?' brought her sister back into reality, back to Bristol and normality. Had she really wanted normality? Probably not, her holiday adventure had been idyllic, extraordinary and absolutely awesome.

Asking what time it was, Jackie jumped out of bed, well not literally, after being informed that it was two-thirty in the afternoon. How had she managed to sleep from early evening the day before until well into the afternoon the following day? Her sleep regime hadn't followed that pattern for years. Rising late most mornings at home hadn't been because of a continual unbroken sleep but the exact opposite. The holiday must have made its mark on her, all in a good way.

She wasn't sure how many times she apologised to her sister, unbelieving of the time elapsed and frightening her sister half to death. Claire had been concerned as to whether she was indeed okay. Unusual as it was, Jackie felt so much better after an unbroken night in bed. A virtually unknown entity, the rare occurrence had been very welcomed. It would have been better if she'd been in her own home, eliminating her sister's fears, though.

Several cups of tea followed after getting up. A soak in a hot bath and dressing in comfortable clothing sealed the day, well, what was left of it. The remainder of the evening was spent relaxing and watching television; all low-key after an adventure filled with activity-based days and evenings, lots of them. Definitely a chill out after a few weeks of highs and even highers! Experience is a good thing, so the saying goes and Jackie was there agreeing wholeheartedly with the words echoing in her head.

Whether there was more to come for Claire's sister in the future, was unknown to her as yet.

Hopefully, there was; Jackie wasn't ready for retirement, even though she was now officially retired.

Her body was giving up but her mind was as alert as ever, most of the time. You're as young as you feel; Jackie and Claire were both young enough to continue their sisterly journeys, weren't they?

Driving back to South Wales alone, Jackie's home held untold memories to treasure. Canada was something else and the company kept, all absolutely brilliant. Mark and Louise were two lucky people, along with their relatives and friends met along the way. Normal people in every way but living in a foreign country, a place that would be recalled regularly in conversations due to the location itself and their lovely personalities; forever friendly, helpful, courteous and obliging.

Everything required in the population of today, well hoped for any roads.

Jackie had been blessed on her sisterly adventure; people, places and perfection on a journey unlikely to be repeated but unique, nevertheless. Beautiful, bewildering and busy; Canada had ticked all the boxes, every one of them. Claire's sister was now back where she belonged but not always where she wanted to be.

Life is never simple. A complicated existence filled with highs and lows along the way whilst growing up, educating each and every human being every minute of the day. Sisters, Claire and Jackie were, having their own individual way of living, lifestyles similar but coping separately in residences far away from each other. Coming together once in a while, their sisterly adventures could continue well into the future. A different location on a different day, but wishes could be granted, hopefully.